Mimsie, Mimsie, Mimsie. Never stop diving into life with the enthusiasm and abandon that you do. It is infectious. I hope you enjoy the book, and it reveals more wonderful gifts, to add **EVERY WOMAN** to the bewitching ones you already have. **A WIT** You're special. You're daft. You're missed already. xxx Chalks.

[07956 920 41]
= me!!
Thanks much for you crazy words, as your wise words!

To our dearest
with love, luck

D0836401

Yes, our Miriam - we adopt you as your English family of sisters so you'd better not forget us! We won't forget you - a wish you all the luck in the world with lasting friendships to carry you through. All love Phoebe xx

Dearest Miriam
I hope you get out of it
We are your words for us
Don't forget us - for us
Surely will not
forget you
keep in touch
Sally xxxx

Miriam, you have special powers, not only in what you see and read, but in the way you make people feel. You are one of life's truely 'beautiful' people. I would be honoured to stay in touch, I hope we do. Enjoy the book.

Books by the Same Author

Psychic Families
Psychic Suburbia
Psychic Power of Children

I Ching Divination for Today's Woman
Moon Divination for Today's Woman

EVERY WOMAN
A WITCH

CASSANDRA EASON

quantum

LONDON • NEW YORK • TORONTO • SYDNEY

quantum

The Publishing House, Bennetts Close,
Cippenham, Berkshire, SL1 5AP, England

ISBN 0-572-02223-9

Typeset in Great Britain by Typesetting Solutions, Slough, Berks
Printed in Great Britain by St Edmundsbury Press Ltd, Bury St Edmunds, Suffolk

CONTENTS

INTRODUCTION

Women can tap natural intuitive powers, not to call up deities from beyond but to focus their own energies to make their everyday lives and relationships easier to handle. What is more, all women, not just those who have adopted a deliberate psychic or spiritual path, have great resources of inner wisdom and an unconscious radar that can pick up cues not available to the conscious mind. Men, too, have these abilities but few, even today, are comfortable relying on intuition.

The old spells of the countryside talk of love, health, money and happiness, and were practised by ordinary people, especially women, everywhere. These have been lost from the everyday world, and the Wiccan movement, with its formal practice of witchcraft, has ironically taken the magic away from the lives of the majority, by its emphasis on obscure gods and strange rituals.

Modern women are faced with the dilemma of having to – do everything – to be career women, home-makers and lovers – and to evolve spiritually. The immaculate models of the cat-walk or advertisements are a million miles from the lives of ordinary women, who may feel pressurised because the image is so far from actuality. It is easy in today's materialistic, achievement-oriented, technological society for women to lose confidence in their own natural magical instincts and deep unconscious wisdom.

Every Woman a Witch gives ancient magical practice a modern everyday, meaningful slant, whether a woman is 15 or 50, alone or in a relationship, successful in the world's terms, or struggling against redundancy and hardship. This book offers no instant happiness, wealth or 'for evers'. Magical action must be followed by real, often painstaking effort in the actual world. Nor does it require expensive and obscure materials, but utilises the contents of home, garden, office and the natural environment.

Each chapter tells the reader what materials are needed and where they can be obtained, and gives detailed steps on how to use them. It is therefore suitable for total beginners to magic. However, because it is not a book of set practices, rather suggestions from which a woman can make her own magical book and methodology, it is intended for those who have already started exploration, but want a new, personalised approach to spirituality.

There is no dabbling with dark powers. The magic used relies on the energies of the natural world and the everyday tools that women would formerly choose spontaneously, before magic and life went their separate ways. This book is for women everywhere, who want something more from their lives and who wish to develop their unique dreams and abilities.

Cassandra Eason

EVERY WOMAN
A WITCH

℘

A re women natural witches? Magic was in times past a natural part of every woman's life. Each village had its wise woman, who knew about herbs and would offer advice on love, relationships and health. The male priest of Christian times did not answer the same need, for he lived apart and did not share the hardships as well as the companionship of ordinary lives.

It is easy to romanticise earlier periods in history and forget the very real difficulties, cruelty, poverty and disease, and the high child mortality rate that persisted even in the early parts of this century. Perhaps that is why magic was so important to women, when issues of life and death were so prevalent and they tried to stave off the harsh fate that frequently threatened their loved ones.

Every woman from Celtic and perhaps earlier times, learned over the centuries – even as outer religious demands changed – the old spells and rituals of the countryside from her own mother, and practised them. She swept out her magic circle as she cleaned her home. While she scrubbed clothes or pots, she would stare deep into the water and see pictures and patterns formed by the suds.

Before tea became a feature of the everyday world (it was introduced into Britain in the mid-seventeenth century, but was a great luxury for many years), every woman read dried herbs or petals from seasonal flowers. She looked into the candle flame as it flickered on the wall in the evening light, or as she sat without sleep by a sick infant's bed. Women interpreted the stones bubbling beneath the stream as they fetched water, and the wind calling from the trees as they gathered wood for the fire.

On the natural lunar and solar festivals men and women would gather and remember the old ways, still alive under the new Christian guise; women were central to these feasts. For example, the old Celtic festival, Brigantia, 31 January, had gradually merged into Candlemas in the Christian calendar. The festival had started in pre-Christian times to celebrate the first ewes' milk available to the tribes after the barrenness of winter. Candles were originally lit to celebrate the joining of the pagan maiden goddess to the corn god. The Celtic Brigid became the Christian St Bride, reputed in medieval legend to be the midwife of Christ. Even today, in remote places, relics of the former pagan ceremony remain, when farmers' wives would place a decorated sheaf of corn in front of the fire as the bride bed, surrounded by candles. Menfolk would be allowed to make a wish on it, in return for a kiss or a gift.

In the mid-fifteenth century, so-called witchcraft became a heresy, and over the following 250 years, almost a quarter of a million people, many of them women, were executed for witchcraft in Europe and later America.

With this persecution, the wise woman and the open practice of magic by women died out. However, girls still continued to practise the old love spells at the time of agricultural festivals, even after the Industrial Revolution drove them into the towns. The herbal healing remedies, increasingly found to have scientific validity, and family divination continued in secret. Granny often took the place of the wise woman, reading the leaves or turning playing cards before an important family event, though she might claim divine inspiration or advice from the spirits. The sound counsel she dispensed came from her own inner wisdom and intuitive understanding of humankind.

The repealing of the Witchcraft Act in 1951 led to the establishment of Wicca, the formal practice of witchcraft. However, this is a mixed blessing, for although Wicca is a form of nature worship with many ecological strengths, it divorces natural magic from everyday life. Most women do not wish to practise formal rites in secret, again handing superior power to high priestesses and priests, and learning rituals created by others that are not the magic of the hearth, the home and the bed.

What is more, the marginalisation of magic confirms the natural division between logic and intuition, instead of seeing them as two parts of a creative whole. From Locke and the Age of Reason, from the latter part of the seventeenth century, through the Industrial Revolution to the present age of science and technology, women have learned to mistrust their basic instincts and inspirations, and in our own times, to listen to the voices of experts and not to their invariably accurate inner voice.

Yet female magic has continued, almost automatically,

revealed spontaneously by the power to sum up someone new in five seconds flat, to get from A to Z without ten pages of working out in between, or to warn a partner to take the train instead of the car. We use our gut feelings, instincts and inspirations unconsciously every day. Most women know the sex of their unborn child without a scan. Many sit bolt upright in bed seconds before a baby wakes, even if there are no regular feeding times, the baby's cot is down the corridor, and the woman is so tired she could sleep through an earthquake. I've heard of fathers who can do the same thing, but it's much rarer. Women especially will phone their mother, who lives at the other end of the country, only to find the telephone engaged as she is trying to get through to them.

ARE WOMEN MORE INTUITIVE
THAN MEN?

We all have powers of logic and intuition, but women do tend to be more aware of their instincts, and closer to the signals that provide information beyond even the non-verbal level of communication. This is not to say that women are superior, and modern education may produce a generation of men who will acknowledge their intuitions more openly; I know many men find my women's divination books useful. However, many men do tell me that they still rely on a female partner's gut feelings and intuitions. A successful female executive of a media firm told me, 'Men have networking in business, women have intuition'.

Having researched psychic experience and divination around the world for several years, I do find that women are more willing to talk about their psychic experiences and rely on their inspirational powers, especially in crises. For every example of paternal intuition, I have a hundred of mothers' foresight.

WHY SHOULD WOMEN NEED MAGIC
IN THE MODERN WORLD?

The choices and opportunities facing modern women are endless, but they can bring uniquely female dilemmas. It's not just a question of juggling a career with the demands of a family, although that is still a major problem. As a working mother with five children and a partner who is frequently absent, I can end up hoovering at midnight and feeling intensely guilty because my children go to school in odd socks.

'Having it all' can sometimes seem like doing it all – and wondering where the 'identity' bit went ... With current 'care in the community' policies, women in middle-age and beyond can find that the needs of an elderly or sick relation must be fitted into an already busy life; indeed many women have always assumed this role. With the loss of the larger extended family, spontaneous childcare and support for elderly family members has largely disappeared. Statistics show that for whatever reason, women rather than men tend to take on the practical business of caring.

Young women may discover that equality was fine in the classroom, but that there are still firms where a pretty face can open doors more easily than competence, and that a male boss may expect his female PA to act as mother, nurse and guardian of his ego.

Women who concentrate on a career can also end up, quite illogically, feeling a failure, because in the eyes of the conventional world, they didn't become a whiter-than-white mum of the adverts, with 1.8 children, an accountant husband and a detached home in the suburbs. Of course such stereotypes aren't valid, but when your mum gets out her copy of *Good Grandparents* and starts to invite twice-divorced male schoolfriends from your primary school for dinner every time you're home, you can feel threatened.

Lone men are still sometimes regarded as 'playing the field', even if they have a beer paunch like an ostrich egg and three failed marriages behind them. A lone woman, however confident or successful, can still have a lingering sense of failure as she takes her bag of groceries home to an empty flat, or jogs around the park alone for the third weekend running. I've talked to singletons and been one myself, and though I knew logically that the world wasn't like Noah's Ark, with the world walking two by two, on a wet Sunday afternoon in suburban London it seemed I was the only dodo left on earth.

Few women avoid a mild dose of the 'empty nest syndrome' in their mid- or late-thirties. A woman with or without a permanent relationship may find a partner who is willing to share the upbringing of a child with her. She may decide to rear a child solo, or not to become a mother. Whatever her decision, the maternal dilemma is not easily solved. The most equal male partner can occasionally turn into Old Father Traditionalist when his partner starts chewing coal and craving strawberry pizzas at 3 am.

I've talked to women all over the western world, in Europe, the USA, Australia and New Zealand – secretaries, singers, film directors, accountants, women in publishing and journalism, carpenters, plumbers and sales assistants. All women have secret dreams, to be a champion swimmer, to write a best seller, to stay at home and bring up a family full time, or to live solo and tend the garden. Most talk of a deep desire to find the right partner, perhaps after the failure of a long-term relationship. This is why this book centres around relationships and family issues. The hardest part of women's lives is not to achieve success in a chosen field; it is to resolve our caring, nurturing, home-making side, which is as rich a part of female nature as it was for our mothers, grandmothers and great-grandmothers. We also have that deep intuitive well of 'unconscious wisdom' as Jung called it – access to the collective wisdom of womankind and mankind in all times and places. But it is hard to trust those inner promptings.

For most women life, like magic, is people-centred. Whether I am doing divinatory readings or just talking, the conversation invariably goes back to the 'people' aspect of work, home and leisure. Of course it happens with men too, but many seem to compartmentalise diverse areas of their lives more strongly than women do. With women it is usually part of the same experience. Therefore many of the rituals and spells in this book are centred around the personal rather than more abstract realms.

The older we get in a society where youth and immature beauty are revered, the more we need to know that our inner loveliness and wisdom are of value. Whether we are struggling to care for elderly parents, becoming a grandmother for the first time, or facing the future alone or as part of a finite partnership, it's vital to rejoice in our ageing process and not try to stand still or go back to an earlier phase.

So let's reclaim our natural magic, and we can have, not everything, but a sense of being in control and powerful in a very female, exciting way. You don't need to join a coven or alter your lifestyle radically. True female magic is best done alone or with a few close female friends, whether at home, at work or out of doors, and it works just as well in the most mundane setting, using the tools and ornaments of our everyday world.

CELANDINE

WHAT IS MAGIC?

Every time we blow out a candle on a birthday cake we are carrying out magic to send our wishes into the cosmos. When we eat a piece of lettered birthday cake, we are taking into ourselves the good wishes it bears. This began among the worshippers of Artemis, the Greek moon goddess; cakes in the shape of the crescent moon would be decorated with candles on her day. Each time we 'touch wood', we are recalling the old Druidic practice of contacting the tree spirits.

People imagine that magic must be practised on windy moorlands with pentagrams and wands. Real magic can be used anywhere, however, with whatever you can find or easily buy.

Modern magic may sometimes be practised in natural places where we feel close to the wind, the rain and the sunshine, but it can equally be practised in the office or at the kitchen sink. There is no need to try to recreate the imagined symbols of witchcraft; just use everyday tools and objects as our forebears would have done. The modern equivalent of the broom is the hoover – more of that later. But first try a form of modern magic based on the old forms.

Linked with spells are divination and scrying – ways of looking at the shape of something, or turning over cards or symbols such as runes with set markings that have traditional meanings – not to tell the future but to get in touch with the unconscious wisdom that can point to potential not considered. Many a maiden of myth, combing her hair by a pool, was looking in the water for images, ripples, cloud patterns or sudden sunbeams that would reflect her inner knowledge in pictorial form.

BEGINNING MAGIC: AUSPICY
(DIVINATION BY BIRD FLIGHT)
IN THE MODERN WORLD

Balloon magic

Balloon magic relates to the ancient traditions of auspicy. It combines the ancient magical elements of fire and air. From earliest times mankind equated the sky with the gods, whom it visualised living in high regions, such as Asgard in the Norse tradition, a glorious region near the top of Yggdrasil, the world ash tree. The Greek gods, with Zeus at their head, lived on

Mount Olympus. The whole principle of offerings therefore relied on sending gifts and prayers upwards to win the favour of the deities.

In the Chinese tradition the sky represented pure *yang*, sometimes pictured as the great dragon in the sky, and in oriental tradition coloured streamers and kites were released, bearing entreaties skywards.

The principle behind balloon magic is to free your wishes or decisions from their earthly bounds in a magical rush of energy. Of course, you then have to use the impetus to make things happen on the earthly plain, but the ritual provides the symbolic impetus for any enterprise.

Birds were regarded in Ancient Greece and Rome as messengers of the gods or even a deity in disguise, and so became an important form of early divination. Apollo often took an eagle's form, while in Ancient Egypt the hawk was regarded as the soul of Horus and the Pharaoh. Decisions were made by looking at the signs in the sky.

Balloons can equally act as a magical focus for divination or spells. You may enjoy going out to a windy hillside with a string of coloured balloons, with children, your own or those of friends. Alternatively, go with a friend and take one or two silver helium balloons, perhaps decorated with hearts for a love matter, gold circles for money, cherubs for fertility or children, flowers for friendship or a new enterprise, cars or planes for travel. If you go to a market stall or card/gift shop you will be amazed by the selection of designs. Pick one or two that seem to represent your goal or problems. The balloons will tug at the string as you carry them along; it is a good way of recalling laughter and fun.

Balloon colour

In traditional magic, different colours can be used for different desires, and balloon colour is a good way of using the old ideas. It may be that you decide to take a rainbow balloon or a whole selection of colours if the issue concerning you is very far-reaching, or you want to integrate different aspects of your life. You will find these colour meanings throughout the book, but you may find that you develop colours that have more personal associations. There are many differences even in traditional lists, and it is a mistake to accept tradition if it does not feel right for you.

White is for anything to do with children or babies, new ventures or beginnings, whether in love or business.

Black is for letting go of old sorrows, grief or guilt, and for problems with older people.

Brown is for practical issues, for home and animals.

Pink is for reconciliation, friendship and health.

Red is for fertility, survival issues and passion.

Orange is for identity issues, for personal happiness and partnerships, whether at home or at work.

Yellow is for communication, for undeveloped potential, for career and for travel.

Green is for any matter of the heart, for romance, marriage and family.

Blue is for learning, examinations, interviews and matters of principle.

Purple is for wisdom, for the soul and spirit, and for religious insight of any kind.

Silver is for dreams, for special wishes and major inner-life changes.

Gold is for translating life-changing plans into reality.

Balloon divination

You may wish to use appropriate balloon colours or for divination use black to represent 'No' or 'Wait', white for 'Yes' or 'Act'. Should you see a flock of birds you can of course follow the ancient art of auspicy.

Divination by balloon direction

Take a balloon and launch it into the sky, while thinking of an endeavour about which you are undecided.

If your balloon veers to the left, your enterprise may have difficulties that you haven't acknowledged but need to think through. If the balloon flies to the right it should be 'plain sailing', so trust your natural instincts to go ahead.

If your balloon goes directly upwards and flies high, so will you – so perhaps raise your sights or your price. If your balloon flies horizontally away from you, you have to make sure that you don't lose out by hesitating or constantly changing your mind or plans.

A sudden change of direction means that you should beware of sneaky dealings, to which you may have closed your eyes.

If your balloon bursts you need to rethink your goal, and if it gets stuck in trees or on objects you'll know there will be an obstacle or two, but that it is important to persevere.

The higher your balloon flies initially, the more likely you are to succeed.

So where does this wisdom come from? Not from the ancient deities, but from that deep well of wisdom we all have, the unconscious radar whose warnings and advice we ignore as it runs round our head. Now the wisdom is projected into the balloon flight, showing you what is just out of range of your consciousness and physical vision.

Deciding between two choices

Decide on the two main choices. Release two balloons at the same time, a 'Yes' and 'No' balloon, and the one to fly straight up the highest gives you the answer. Watch the course of the balloons for the long-term effect. You may find one course is only effective in the short-term. If it is a question of following your head or heart, you could release a blue and a green balloon.

If there are three options, use three balloons.

I have used this technique many times with different people and it invariably proves accurate. It does not rely on wind direction, for balloons released a minute later do not follow an identical path since the situation has been changed by the initial asking.

A balloon spell to release a wish

Write your wish on a long piece of paper, the colour of your wish, e.g. green paper if you want to travel. As you write your secret desire, see yourself free from doubt and fear of failure, and visualise yourself as you are now, but happier, achieving your aim. You can also write down any burdens you may wish to be free of, or unresolved past wrongs that should now be let go. Tie your paper – several if you wish – to the balloon string, and as you let it go, say or shout, if no one is around, 'I am free', 'I have money', 'I have love'; whatever you desire. Young children enjoy this part.

Follow the path of your balloon as far as you can, using the principles of bird-balloon flight to watch the direction and whether it takes straight off and goes upwards; if it does not, you will need to take several steps to succeed and overcome a few obstacles. Now go and have fun, doing something that perhaps you haven't done since a child.

Tonight or tomorrow you will need to translate the wish into earthly action, but for now forget doubt and difficulty, and be joyous.

MAKING YOUR OWN SPELLS

Forget spells demanding 'eye of newt and wing of bat'. Be cautious, too, of ready-packaged mail-order spells or rows of expensive pouches of herbs hanging up at psychic fairs, promising instant love, money and the rest – for a price.

The danger with instant, tailor-made spells is that you'll leave the work entirely to the concoction. For example, sage, whether placed on the forehead or used in a potion, is good for memory, but it won't impart knowledge that isn't there, and once you've spiced up your memory you've still got all the slog of those facts and figures to digest.

A sympathetic practitioner can help you to work out the spell that is best for you, but it is a field wide open to frauds, and ultimately you do the best spells *for* yourself *by* yourself. Mine are only suggestions, and I've left out any ritual chants or words.

There are many beautiful ceremonies in print from both Wicca and more formalised religions. Just as you need no tutor to tell you how to express love, hold a baby or appreciate a sunset, so your own words, whether spoken within or out loud, are there, prompted by the need and emotion that lies behind all spells. Of course you can and should laugh both at yourself, the sheer wonder of nature, and the pomposity of some New Age practitioners who try to make magic an exclusive club for the few instead of the province of all. Magic is full of humour and the day we stop laughing is the day we should quit magic.

1. The aim of a spell

You must have a real need, which need not be grand in the scheme of things. If you've got to get the washing dry or mend the car and need a dry period, then that's just as genuine a need as true love or success on the Stock Market. So if a matter is vital to you, then it's a valid subject.

2. The focus

The main part of any spell involves a ritual to focus your psyche and to generate enough initial power to make the link between the focus of your spell and the actual need or object you desire. This ritual will vary with each person, but you may like to use my ideas for a while until your own creativity takes over.

You can do sympathetic magic, for example, a coin for money – whether you use a penny or dime or some elaborately carved pentacle has more to do with your own preferences and availability. I tend to favour everyday items. This approach depends on like attracting like – Jung's 'synchronicity'.

3. Visualisation

Summoning up in your mind's eye, focusing on a desired future person or object as 'here and now' in your life, is the essence of any good spell. Visualise yourself as you are right now, not a slimmer, more beautiful or intellectual version of yourself. This is the you driving that new car, sitting in your new house, holding your new baby (we'll leave out the dirty nappy). As you hold the longed-for moment in that present 'out of time', it becomes real, and the power generated can then transform it into external actuality.

However, you can't and definitely should not influence another person's mind or behaviour. That has to be off-limits, or you can easily slip over into the world of mind control and psychic invasion, which is only one step away from psychic attack.

You can change your own mind or behaviour by creative visualisation, such that your impact on others and their perception of you alters. You can make yourself more desirable, assertive, successful in the world's eyes, and this can have the effect of attracting another person or exciting job your way. You can help yourself walk away from a difficult person or situation by actually experiencing the moment in advance internally.

The best changes are always those you make primarily because *you* want the new state. To become something different to please someone else, whether practically or in magical terms, is always risky but, of course, sometimes we think it's worthwhile.

4. Raising the power

You need to raise the magical energies to a crescendo by speaking or moving faster and faster, like a plane taking off on the tarmac, a sprinter on the starting block or a rocket before take-off. A good example of this technique is in *knot magic*.

Take a cord, a ribbon or a piece of string. You may wish to make a single knot or tie nine separate knots with each line of the chant. Nine, the number of the planet Mars and therefore one associated with spiralling energies, has many mythological associations, including the Nine Worlds of Yggdrasil and the nine nights Odin hung from the world tree in Norse cosmology.

As you tie the cord, visualise power rising through your body and from earth and sky, either as a cone, a vortex or as glorious rainbow liquids rising in a crystal phial and cascading into myriad pieces. My own favourite chant involves an adaptation of a very old and popular knot chant, that though originally created for calling up external powers, provides an equally potent focus for personal energies.

> 'By the knot of one, the power's begun,
> By the knot of two, the power's renewed,
> By the knot of three, my power's in me,
> By the knot of four, the power is more,
> By the knot of five, the power's alive,
> By the knot of six, my fate's not fixed,
> By the knot of seven, the power is leaven,
> By the knot of eight, I make my fate,
> By the knot of nine, the power is mine.'

'The power is free.' Undo your knots and each time recite 'The power is free' in a crescendo of sound. Cast the cord into a fast-flowing stream or into candle flame, for it has served its purpose. If you use a silk scarf you will not wish to destroy it, so throw it high so it catches the breeze.

5. Letting the magic go

Whether you cast a star into the cosmos, release a balloon, blow out a candle or untie a knot, all magic has a moment of release, of letting go, when all that magical energy leaves the object or you. If you do this you'll not only give the energies a chance to work, but will stop that buzzing of unfocused energy in your head. Sometimes the letting go will be quite subtle, a phrase in your head, a flower cast into water, the completion of a circle. However, that is not the end, rather the beginning.

6. Action

Real magic, as opposed to the 'power-trip' kind, often flounders when it comes to using that power as a basis for action in the real world. Once you've got your magical energies ticking over and have blown out your candle or cast your flowers in the water, you've then got the less exciting but vital part to carry out.

Perhaps that's why so many magical practitioners are dreamy, ethereal creatures who are always doing spells rather than using them to improve the here and now. It's like learning to drive in a field and never venturing out on to a road. So after your candle is reduced to wax and your flowers are stuck in a litter trap at the side of the pond, you have got to go out and read those books, say those words, whether 'I love you' or 'Goodbye'. You've got to keep on studying the manuals, unravelling the oily bits of the combustion engine, swimming lap after boring lap to improve your timings, or even day after day carrying out the routine care of someone who depends on you.

FINALLY . . .

Never hex, curse or even think of someone with hostility while you are doing magic of any kind, tempting though it may be, and justifiable though it may seem. I'm not into mass forgiveness, but many people who do wrong or are spiteful or vicious ultimately end up sad, lonely and very unhappy because of their own behaviour.

It's not easy to avoid doing magic with bad feeling in your heart if you are hurt, rejected or plain angry. However, it's as well to leave your spells until you are feeling more positive.

Psychic attacks can happen quite unconsciously, but any form of negative magic you initiate will give you a headache or something rather worse.

If you want to sock someone on the nose do it on the material plane, and afterwards read a book or hammer some nails until you are back in balance.

DO YOU NEED PROTECTION WHEN DOING SPELLS?

In traditional magic either archangels or one or more aspects of the Goddess are often invoked to protect the corners of a magical working. However, practitioners with more enthusiasm than sense sometimes go on to invoke all kinds of forces, and draw powers into themselves they scarcely understand and cannot control. It's like touching wood. We all do it, though we aren't usually calling on friendly tree spirits for aid.

If you do bad magic to hurt other people or to end up with a lot of power or material goodies yourself, then bad vibes will fly round and affect you not only during the spell but afterwards. Protection, whether from psychic or psychological threats, comes only from positive thoughts and altruistic actions. You will automatically tap into whatever benign force or natural powers lie behind existence. If you do any kind of psychic or spiritual work, whether divination, spells or visualisation, it's important to put in what you seek to take out, and to keep your feet on the ground before, during and after your spells.

Fortunately, magic has its own inbuilt limiting factor to stop you drifting off to other realms, and by using everyday tools and objects you aren't tempted to get off on a psychic ego trip and forget the real action within you that is needed for success.

YOUR MAGICAL TOOLS

You've got most of these already in the kitchen drawer, garden shed or around the house or office. Real magic starts where you are and from what you are. You don't need costly wands, pentacles or altar cloths, because that is to remove magic from reality.

Children know that the box is often the most exciting part of a toy, but the world teaches us that it is the cost of the goods that matters. Improvisation is the gift of the infant. Purpose-made perfection screams from every advertisement. So we spend so much time trying to make our worlds tone and blend, and discovering expensive new gadgets for the simplest chore, that we lose touch with our own ingenuity and creativity.

Work colleagues, flatmates and family won't mock your magical tools if they don't realise they are out of the ordinary. They should not be. Tools are tools, whether for digging the garden, mending a fuse or making magic. The power is within.

It can be a bit disconcerting to see your eldest child dressing up in what passes as your altar cloth, or your flatmate draining the vegetables through your sacred water sprinkler, but we aren't practising our craft outside the world, but right in the middle of the action or current quagmire. That's our secret and the way we are likely to succeed.

It's as well to keep at least one foot on the ground. Magic is only frightening if it becomes divorced from reality and our own natural, instinctive abilities. A new-born infant is perhaps the most wonderful, magical, miraculous creature of all. Spirituality is simplicity, based on love and laughter. Every woman, whether working as president of an international bank, as a captain of industry, watching butterflies or caring for an incapacitated relative, shares the magical inheritance of queen and peasant woman, and carries the secrets to future generations.

MAGICAL TOOLS

Magic begins in the home, whether a flat, a bedsit, a room in your parents' house, a suburban semi, a luxury urban penthouse or a remote country cottage. Like your home, your magical tools will reflect your personality, whether you prefer a functional decor, a comfortably cluttered atmosphere or a more exotic setting. Your own furniture, objects and personal trinkets are endowed with your essence; they are grounded in the real person that is your core, whether you are thirteen, thirty or eighty. Therefore they bring to ritual and divination a unique power, not present in magical tools bought or made by others especially for spells.

A MAGICAL PLACE

Choose a shelf over a fireplace, the top of a cupboard, a spare table or your dressing table for a working surface. You may like to keep it decorated with flowers, leaves or berries of the passing seasons and a gold and silver candle, perhaps candlesticks that you have bought on a happy occasion or were given by a friend or family member. I have a sun and moon metal pair, and keep a silver candle for the moon and a gold one for the sun, the ancient female and male symbols.

This serves as a magical working place when you are alone. The word 'altar' seems wrong for me, as it is a place where I keep my favourite crystals, any special pebbles I find on a walk, cards or special letters I am sent, and I am quite happy for the children to play with the crystals and pebbles. For me, it is a family place, and we light the candles sometimes for a quiet end to the day. However, others may prefer to keep it separate from other people.

A TREASURE BOX

I keep a few things I know I often use for magic in a large plastic box with a lid. Others may prefer a special box, perhaps covered with fabric or special paper, or an old wooden box. It need not be large, just big enough for candles, incense sticks, a little container of salt, some metal foil, matches etc. Over the months you will find your box contains objects that reflect your own ideas. (*See* Chapter 11 for ideas and uses for your treasure box.)

ELEMENT SYMBOLS

These are not chemical elements in the scientific sense, but the ancient symbolic elements of which life was once believed to consist, and to which Jung gave psychological attributes. I keep some of these in my magical place and some in my magic box, but substitutes can easily be found around the home or office.

Earth is traditionally associated with practical, material issues and a step-by-step approach, with returning to the real, essential, root self. This element is situated in the north and is associated with winter; you might, like me, need to use a map or compass to find your directions, but some people instinctively know where north is. For some practitioners it is vital that you use accurate compass positions. For others the directions are more symbolic, and an approximation serves as well. If you are in the office or a busy place it may not be practical to start finding exact positions, and as I say many, many times, symbolism is a tool, not a mistress. It may be less confusing to think of north as the 12 o'clock position.

Salt in a dish, or a small canister of salt, is ideal for earth magic. Alternatively you can fill a dish with pot-pourri or any other dried flower petals as your earth symbol. Witches' houses are remarkably fragrant places. If you have nothing instantly available, an apple, vegetable or coin provides an earth symbol.

Air represents logic and the mind. It is a symbol for change, sometimes with strife, but often simply involving an effort to alter the status quo. The sky can be the limit. Air is the element of spring, and goes in the east in the 3 o'clock position.

Incense sticks are excellent for air magic; I keep a selection of different flower fragrances in my box. A needle or small paper knife are also symbolic. However, you can equally well use an environmentally friendly air freshener, ideal for a quick air spell when you are not alone.

Fire speaks of the sun, of creativity, inspiration and communication, and all those wonderful leaps to the stars. Fire goes in the south in the 6 o'clock position. This is the element of summer.

Candles are perfect for fire magic. I keep a pack of small household candles in my box. The flame from a lighter, a box of matches or even the ring of a gas stove or a make-up mirror, placed to catch the light, will serve equally well.

Water involves feelings and intuition, going with the flow, moving forwards and not clinging on to what has gone, being aware of what is going on under the surface. It is found in the west in the 9 o'clock position, and is associated with autumn.

A vase of flowers or a dish of water with a few crystals or petals floating in it are ideal in your magical place. You could follow tradition and leave this ceremonial water in the sunlight and the moonlight for 24 hours, to absorb solar and lunar vibes.

I keep a bottle of still mineral water in my box for quick spells. However, if you are in a hurry or in public, a glass or cup of tap water or even a paper cup of coffee works as well. The magic is within; the lovely candles and crystals may make us feel more magical, but they are not essential.

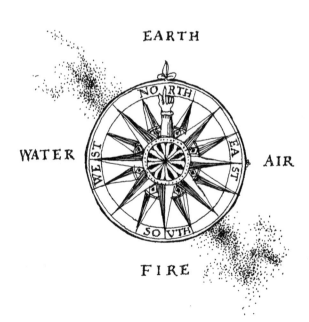

EARTH

WATER

AIR

FIRE

THE MAGIC CIRCLE

A circle is a basic shape in elemental magic. The centre is a combination of all four of the ancient elements, making a fifth element sometimes called 'ether', sometimes 'akasha', that is supposed to be different from and greater than the others, the ideal goal or state. In psychology it is often associated with Jung's 'inner child'.

You may wish to keep circles of different sizes and colours in your box. I use silver cooking foil as a basic circle; silver is the colour of the moon, and aluminium the metal of Mercury, planet and deity of communication. However, you can make a circle with thread, draw one in chalk or crayon on A4 paper, or visualise one and draw it in the air or on the table. Traditionally you draw a circle clockwise or deosil (sunwise), and when you have finished your spell you retrace it with your finger or in your mind, or, if thread, unwind it in a moonwise or anti-clockwise direction.

SIMPLE SPELL-MAKING USING THE ELEMENTS

What is your current aim or particular problem? Choose something that concerns you, however irrelevant or seemingly trivial to others. You can choose an issue or goal at work, in relationships or at home, or to do with yourself. Start with a simple concern if you wish, and work up to major life changes. However, since spells work when focused on need and endowed with emotion, the spell should be personal.

Create a circle in your mind, draw one on paper or make one with thread. Place four element symbols in the four main compass positions, and in the centre a symbol of your goal, perhaps a credit card or coin for money, a flower or two small dolls for love, a toy car or plane or ticket for travel, a tiny tool or pen for career or learning. I keep a whole selection of tiny toys and trinkets in my box, or you can put tiny ornaments in your magical place.

Hold your symbol, whether of travel, love or money, in your left hand for right-brain intervention (the left hand is controlled by the right side of the brain, and vice versa). In turn, pass it through the four elements, beginning in the north.

As you pass slowly through the north, see the practical steps you will take to achieve your dream. In the east, see added the logic and thought that will ensure you succeed. As you slowly pass through the south, feel the glow of inspiration rise, and finally in the west, let your heart stir with excitement as the four elemental powers flower in a mighty stream to carry you back to the north.

Return your symbol to the centre, and in your mind or with your finger or a pencil trace backwards round the circle anti-clockwise, seeing the power flying free. You may like to say words such as, 'The power is free, the spell is free', whatever feels right for you. Visualise the energy as a star, a sunbeam, a rainbow.

Take your symbol and carry it with you through the day, or, if the spell takes place in the evening, sleep with it beneath your pillow. As soon as possible, take a first step towards making your dream come true, perhaps in the practical earth sphere if that is easiest.

Element spells do not have to be practised so formally, however. You may wish to begin with a simple circle spell, and then repeat it creatively at home or out of doors, as Emma did.

• Emma works in a successful electrical engineering partner-ship with Gill, a woman she met at college. However, she and her partner have fallen out over the apprentice they want to take on as part of a Government scheme. Emma feels strongly that another woman would fit in best and wants to give girls a chance to work in a field where initially she encountered strong prejudice. Gill says Emma is being sexist, however; she thinks they should appoint the best person for the job regardless of sex, and thinks a man would balance the 'all-girls-together' atmosphere that Emma sees as supportive, but she sometimes finds stifling.

Two candidates, a man and a woman, seem equally suited, and Emma wants to take on the woman. However, Gill says they should give it to the man in the interests of equality. The discussion degenerates into a slanging match in which Emma accuses Gill of needing a man around to flatter her ego, and Gill accuses Emma of clinging to her because she has problems relating to men. They are now barely speaking, and have to make a decision within a couple of days.

Emma decides to use a bit of magic to restore harmony to their working environment and friendship. The workshop is at the back of her home, so she goes through into the kitchen and cuts out a tinfoil circle. In the middle she puts a small pastry cutter in the shape of her heart, for friendship.

She passes the pastry cutter over a small canister of salt in the north, a small perfume spray in the east, the silver lid of some gravy granules, that catches the light, in the south, and her half-finished orange juice in the west. She feels that as she sips from the glass, part of her essence is within. As she passes the symbol round she sees the common sense of earth putting the quarrel into perspective, the logic of what is best emerging from the east, the need for an innovative solution as the key in the south, and her natural affection flowing in the west.

Emma still does not have a clear answer, however, so she goes for a walk to allow her elemental insights to merge. First she goes to the lake in the park for her *watery* environment, for she realises it is important to look beneath the surface to the real problem. This, she realises, with her new magical insight, is less about choosing a male or female apprentice, and more to do with what she and Gill each seek from their working relationship and friendship.

Emma sees a pink rose that has been picked and cast aside. She identifies pink as symbolising reconciliation, and the rose as a symbol of the underlying empathy between her and Gill. The rose represents the *earth* element, going back to the root of the matter and using her basic senses to re-establish the real priorities, which angry words have displaced. Roses are traditionally symbols of love and fidelity.

As Emma casts each petal into the water she visualises Gill and sends her positive thoughts. At the same time she plays the childhood game, and for each petal says, 'Boy', 'Girl', 'Boy', 'Girl', until finally she is left with a single petal. As she goes to throw it, however, the petal splits in half and the answer comes into Emma's head, 'Take on both candidates.'

But how? They probably wouldn't job-share, and the firm cannot afford both. She also realises that the splitting petal is a sign that the 'two-some' has become claustrophobic, and by excluding men from her working and emotional life after a long-standing relationship broke up in bitterness, she herself has been making a restrictive environment. Often the insights we receive when doing magic can hold the key to deeper reasons for seemingly illogical prejudices.

On her way back to her workshop/home, Emma sees a small poster from the local college and stops to read it. It is advertising a joint on-the-job training/college scheme, and asks firms as well as students to apply for details. There are grants for participating firms.

Waiting on Emma's desk is a bunch of roses the exact pink of the one Emma cast into the water. Gill has left a note saying that if it is really important to Emma to give the job to a girl, she will go along with it, since the girl is well qualified for the position.

Emma and Gill get two for the price of one through the college scheme, the two apprentices work well together, and Emma and Gill are now participating in the college scheme regularly.

Coincidence? Telepathy? Or earth and water magic bringing two people back together? We can't measure magic or guarantee eternal happiness or riches. But we can strengthen and utilise our inner wisdom so that we do take the right steps at the moment when success or reconciliation is most likely. If, as Jung believed, we all share a collective, unconscious reservoir of knowledge and wisdom, perhaps we can make enough ripples in our spells to affect the outer as well as our inner world in a positive way.

A MAGIC WAND

Of course you need one. Remember all those fairy godmothers in the best stories? – one wave and pumpkins turn into golden coaches and frogs into handsome princes (though maybe, like me, you'd prefer a home help to do the dishes). You can go into the woods and cut yourself a hazel wand (the tree of wisdom), which you can keep in a display of leaves and flowers in your living room. This can double for dowsing (more of that and other divinatory skills in Chapter 10).

You may, however, prefer to purchase a piece of clear crystal quartz as your wand, pointed and clear at one end for all those positive 'go-for-it' energies, and rounded and cloudy at the other for receptive, intuitive, empathetic powers. It need not be more than a few inches long and should not cost very much – try a well-lit New Age shop with clear displays you can handle, or a mineral store. Many larger department stores also sell clear quartz. If possible, buy the real thing; lead or rainbow crystal is not any cheaper, and lacks the natural energies of real crystal quartz. Don't worry if your crystal has a few impurities or flaws. It is said that such crystals contain angels and fairies.

If you need a bit of energy, hold the clear pointed end outwards and see yourself catapulted forward into a tunnel of brilliant light. If you need some calm, point the clouded rounded end towards you and be cocooned in soft cotton wool clouds. The first method is good for getting you going in the morning or when you've got an important meeting or date. The second is good for helping you to sleep, or calming you if you're feeling jittery. It's a good idea to keep your wand near your bedside.

MAKING THE HOME
PSYCHICALLY FRIENDLY

You go into some houses, apartments or mobile homes and immediately sense underlying peace and harmony. Of course the family argue, the children fight, music blares and the cats spit, but there is a deep underlying warmth and feeling of security and familiarity that makes you reluctant to leave.

Psychic harmony doesn't depend on tidiness or elegance, though you may find that the mess of others does irritate you and makes you feel unsettled. In this case define what is acceptable to you (not to mother-in-law or the ladies on the adverts with their gleaming mop buckets), and set an approximate outer order. If you live alone, harmony at home and a welcoming atmosphere are especially important in creating a haven where your rich inner world can find expression.

This deep inner peace marks out the territory, whether caravan or castle, as a place of happiness and love. The Chinese use the ancient art of *feng shui* (wind and water), and surveyors in the Orient are often followed by *feng shui* experts to see if a site is harmonious in terms of the underlying *yang/yin* balance that is necessary for the benefits of *ch'i*, the universal life force that flows through all existence. As well as contours, the presence or absence of water, the shape of buildings and even where furniture is placed in a room can be crucial.

The essential principle is that natural contours should be followed. In China, owners of businesses as well as homes try to increase the harmony of a building; for example, a small mirror and wind chimes are placed at the door to deflect bad fortune and evil spirits.

Modern dowsers in the West sometimes say they detect black streams under buildings, which are supposed to be related to ill-health or unhappiness in the occupants. They believe these can often be deflected by inserting balancing metal rods in various parts of the home.

There are many ways you can make your home 'feel right', and thus encourage positive relationships and attract others to your sanctum of calm. This deliberate fostering of tranquillity works well with children, who can become less hyperactive and quarrelsome if they feel in tune with a place. It has been shown that certain colours, such as pink, in an institution such as a prison or mental hospital have a calming effect. However, we all instinctively have colours that either resonate or jar, and this is a personal relationship, so if you hate pink it is not likely to increase your sense of well-being.

LIVING OASES OF CALM

If you share your living space, your home environment is likely to be filled with activity and movement. Or perhaps you are alone, whether by choice or circumstance, and in spite of music or the sound of television or radio, the silence whirls round and the disembodied voices aren't those you want to hear. In either case you can bring harmony to your home by creating oases of calm, areas of the room, house or flat to which you are instinctively drawn, and where your tensions and doubts fade away.

Cats

Cats always choose the best place in a home to sit, the sunniest corner by day and the softest, warmest niche by night. If you have a cat, follow his or her patterns, or, provided you don't have an allergy, acquire one or more, and tune into a more serene, rhythmic existence.

Cats were sacred to the Egyptians, who worshipped the cat-headed Bast, guardian of pregnant women, about 3,000 BC, and some people believe that cats are very old, wise souls.

Every witch needs her 'familiar' – forget the myths about black cats being unlucky. This superstition came about after the Nordic people became Christianised in the eleventh century, and the black cats that pulled Freya's chariot suddenly found themselves cast as demons. Any cat will provide a listening ear and a soothing response after a hard day. They aren't like dogs, who are constantly demanding or needing to prove their affection, and who provide love of a different kind. A cat comes when he or she wants you or you need him or her, and the interactions between cats and women are no bad role model for life.

A cat will provide an oasis of quiet and act as a monitor if the vibrations are getting disharmonious. Look to the side of your cat – staring isn't cat-like – and tune into the deep vibrations of an older, slower, more permanent world. You don't even need words; cats are mistresses of telepathy, and often you'll hear an answer to a seemingly impossible dilemma beamed back if you just sit close. You may even get to stroke your cat's fur and be rewarded with a purr, a sound as rich as any conventional mantra.

You don't need a rare pedigree breed or even a kitten. Go to your local cats' home and you'll find row upon row of beautiful adult cats who have experienced the harsher side of life and so will be especially empathetic and wise, once you have proved your own trustworthiness. Take time to talk to them and stroke them – you'll find your cat will pick you and not be at all the one you expected.

If you can't keep cats or don't want to, get a model or two of Ancient Egyptian-type cats. You can often pick them up cheaply at a car boot sale, a craft fair or from a market stall, and they can provide a quiet centre to which you can retreat. Perhaps you could make yourself a pottery cat or choose one of the very simple, fluid, modern designs. Keep these on a low table with a soft rug or cushion nearby so you can sit and talk to your cats when you are alone, or communicate telepathically if your children or flatmates are filling the sound waves. As you communicate in this gentle, intuitive way you can build up a reservoir of quiet wisdom to draw on in time of need.

Fish

The fish is another sacred creature, to the Chinese and to Buddhists everywhere, and in Ancient Egypt the fish was a fertility symbol. Fish are also ancient magical symbols for water.

You don't need exotic tropical specimens; a couple of goldfish in a large tank can offer a focus for gentle meditation and an escape into the gentle environment we last experienced in the womb. Our glinting fish are part of a living crystal ball and can take us to other dimensions, magical lands of sea goddesses and mermaids, and cities now deep under the waves. When the outer world becomes too much we can project ourselves inside those watery caverns. You may like to put a few crystals in the bottom of your tank, and some underwater plants to hide behind when dry land becomes arid or threatening.

Children, too, can be soothed from the jarring world of television by this gentler living screen, where their imagination and psyche can float free. Soft lighting behind the tank can provide a focus for a quiet family time at the end of the day; you can tell legends of cities lost beneath lakes and oceans where the church bell can still be heard tolling. You'll be amazed how many such tales are waiting to be told, from your childhood or perhaps from a deeper well of myth you're tapping into.

Plants and flowers

You can mark the passage of the seasons by your changing flower and leaf display. Display greenery in the winter as a reminder of the midwinter solstice, when early man hung up evergreens to encourage the dead trees to bud again, and lit bonfires to persuade the dying sun to return. Perhaps you'd like to begin around 21 December, the midwinter solstice, in the knowledge that the shortest and darkest day is past. The worst is over and it's almost time to leave your cave, so clear out a bit of the unwanted emotional luggage.

In spring there are daffodils, crocuses, bluebells and sticky buds to recall Ostara, the goddess after whom Easter is named, and the vernal equinox when the lighter days begin. Around 21 March day is equal to night again, and you know that life is budding and blooming and you're not left out of the new beginnings. Primroses traditionally stand for early youth and new beginnings, and the crocus means early joy.

Summer flowers are very cheap, and you don't have to be

a Druid to be aware that by 21 June the summer light is at its height and you should enjoy every moment while you can, and perhaps spend the longest day out of doors. Roses represent perfection and fullness, and any golden flower, even the humble buttercup, talks of inner riches as well as the profusion of nature.

By the autumn equinox, 21 September, you can display fruits and berries as well as dried corn and flowers, to celebrate the gathering in of all our efforts, and assess what went well and what you want in the future. Adam and Eve were supposed to have been given the vine by the angel who turned them out of paradise, and the grape harvest falls at this time.

The much-despised school nature table of childhood held a very important message – that we are all part of the natural world, not above it or beyond it. I use my magical space not only for flowers but for special natural things I find – a bleached stick from the beach, a strangely shaped stone, shells, pots of herbs. It's all too easy, especially if we work indoors and in winter travel in the dark, to become cut off from the natural world and the changing seasons.

In an ideal world we would spend time in the open air, but often weeks go by and we've dashed from car or train to work and then to the supermarket or school. I live about five minutes from the sea, but sometimes I realise that a fortnight has gone by and I haven't taken time to see it – bad for me and even worse for the children.

By holding whatever we have in our natural place we can restore those gentle earth energies that can help us tune into our inner seasons. At the moment I've got some fossilised wood, millions of years old, I found on a local beach. It's full of iron pyrites, fool's gold, a reminder of priorities and that the constant dash to succeed can be a blind alley in terms of personal and professional happiness.

You don't have to have Celtic roots to go back to the old natural ways, for they are as old as mankind itself. However alienated modern people feel from a particular background from which they are descended, we all have our roots in this early pre-culture. This can form the basis for life today, and is just waiting in our window boxes, parks and gardens.

Crystals

Reconciliatory and healing crystals are special sources of tranquillity. Rose quartz, amethyst, blue lace agate and moonstone are cheap and easily obtainable. Hold your rose quartz when you have had a quarrel or feel out of sorts with yourself. Pick amethyst when you have lost sight of what really matters in your life. Blue lace agate is for healing and for gentle courage, not the dragon-slaying kind, but persistence against the odds.

Choose gentle jade for unconditional love for yourself, and when you feel yourself becoming shrill and critical. Buy a brown tiger's eye for common sense, and to remind you to trust your own wisdom, not accept blindly the opinions of others.

If in doubt close your eyes and pick a crystal at random. Whatever colour you choose it will tell you what you need to know and fill you with its gentle, healing energies. Finally find a brown or black pebble and keep it with your other crystals as a reminder of your roots and priorities, and that sometimes the most exciting option isn't the right one.

Candles

Coloured candles or night-lights provide a gentle, magical focus at the end of the day. Scented candles can be floated in water. If you have children, this twilight intersection can provide a door between the flurry of the day and sleep. Research shows that children in the western hemisphere often tend to go to bed crying and over-excited, with parents yelling and equally exhausted. This was found to be very different in slower, tribal life, where calmer rhythms are usual.

Children can, with simple precautions, share in your candle-time, with all the lights dimmed, watching the flickering flames. Candles can be used for divination, a technique which I'll describe later. But for now light your candles, and in the silence let the benign shadows come and go and the smoke carry away all your negative feelings.

Candles link us with an older world where people rose and went to bed by the sun. Alone, with a partner or with a few loved friends, candle-time is a way of tuning into more permanent time patterns.

Pink is the colour of reconciliation and sweet dreams. Purple is for the mystical side we all possess, and silver is the colour of the moon. Dark blue talks of our ideals and the dream we can put in practice, while green is for love and the heart. White puts all these together and promises a new start tomorrow. So if you only have ordinary white kitchen candles, these can be the best of all.

A spell for harmony in the home

Our modern world is so noisy that we are overwhelmed by jagged sounds, and so suffer from headaches, irritability and, with children, hyperactivity. Switch off all electrical appliances that are not vital. Light a soft purple candle and draw the curtains to shut out the noise of cars. Concentrate on letting all those jagged, harsh sounds flow away, and with them the jarring inside your head.

Take cotton wool and in it place a jagged crystal, stone or piece of metal to represent all those jarring sounds inside and outside your head, all the harsh voices, the loud music, the screech of machines. Wrap them in a dark scarf, or even a black sock if you have nothing else, and put them in a drawer.

If you have wind chimes, ring them softly to restore harmony. Finally, set a music box in motion and let the room be filled with gentle sound. If you have children sit by them in the silence while they fall asleep, and let them watch the candle fairies fly.

You may need to wash your crystal or stone many times and replace it in the drawer.

Let some peaceful music restore harmonious rhythm after the spell.

MAKING THE HOME
PSYCHICALLY SAFE

We can all feel under threat. It's not only children who are prey to terrors of the night, and we may feel that someone is sending hostile thoughts towards us. It may be some irresponsible soul who may not even have realised that if you lie fuming about someone you are polluting the psychic atmosphere. It's no consolation that he or she will end up with a monumental headache. Bad vibes are nasty – that's why it's better to make them into stars and let the cosmos deal with them.

If right now you're jittery, have nasty dreams, see shadows in the corners or notice the cat's fur rising, or that he or she takes themselves off for a while, you may feel in need of protection. You can safeguard against any outside negativity, consciously or unconsciously projected your way, and neutralise any bad feeling that comes with family, partner or visitors.

THE PROTECTIVE SENSES

Animals use all their senses to detect danger. We are less developed in this way, so need to awaken our own inner protective devices.

Sound and hearing

Buy some wind chimes, preferably with a couple of crystals attached, to place near your outer doors or in your kitchen. This is harnessing the *air element* as well as creating harmonious sound to counteract any angry words or thoughts that come your way. Musical door chimes work on the same principle, provided the tune is harmonious. Don't be surprised if your wind chimes make a sound when there is little breeze; it's just those protective energies on psychic patrol.

Light and sight

Like the Chinese you can use a mirror – we borrowed the wind chimes from them – again facing the door. You can hang up a couple of stainless steel saucepans or a wok on the kitchen wall to the same effect. The mirror is seen as casting light to repel darkness. This is using the *fire element* as well as light. Crystals hanging around catch the light beautifully, and cast rainbows on the floor and walls, or you can buy those perspex stained-glass window-shapes, or make your own.

Fragrance – the sense of smell

Animals use this sense to provide all kinds of information. You can waft your favourite perfume spray to good effect, especially if it is a fragrance you have worn for some months and so has strong associations with you. An environmentally-friendly air deodoriser block, fresh herbs such as lemon balm or apple mint, flowers or pot-pourri can work just as well, and at night you can burn incense before going to bed. You are spoiled for choice in the *earth element* department.

Taste

Use water steeped in peppermint in saucers, or small dishes of rose water on your window ledges, to provide a psychic moat around the entry points. Garlic is also traditionally proof against nasties and things that go bump in the night, but not all people welcome this fragrance as a permanent resident.

Touch

You can if you wish use a rough-cut protective crystal such as tiger's eye, coral, jade, lapis lazuli (the eye of the gods), carnelian, jet, amber and clear quartz. Keep this close to your bed, or put it in a pocket or bag that you carry.

If you can trace around the outer walls of your home physically, use your crystal to make an invisible, unbroken line around it in the air about six inches away from the actual building. If you live in a flat or bedsit three floors up, visualise the exterior points, encircle it with a golden force field, and see all who live inside protected with the circle or a golden pyramid of light.

To protect individual rooms, begin in the north of each one and touch each corner with a sprinkling of salt. Go round again with the fragrance of an incense stick or your air freshener, thirdly with a candle or torch circled clockwise, and finally with a few drops of rose water made by soaking rose petals, for harmony. As you use each element visualise the power of solid stone ramparts, rushing wind, the sun and the mighty sea, protecting your home space.

Try to make the rest of the day or evening harmonious, and as quiet as possible. Do something positive – tidy a drawer, clear away cobwebs (so long as you ask the spider if she doesn't mind), even paint a scuffed skirting board or wall.

Open the windows if it is sunny. If you have children forget their untidy bedrooms – they will be there tomorrow and the day after Judgement – and spend time with them. Go for a walk, read or just talk. It's a good time to get out the old photos and talk to family or friends about the happy times and the disasters, or if you are alone, to relive the fond memories in your mind's eye. It's especially important with children to harmonise with the past, so make it a time to bake Gran's or Great-gran's favourite recipes, and share the old family legends. You may even feel a departed elderly relative around, or smell their favourite perfume. Whether or not you believe such things are possible, you can still invoke happy memories and their positive, protective powers.

If there are any family quarrels this might be a good day to extend the olive branch. Even if it is not accepted, you have made a positive step and freed yourself. End the day by lighting a pink, purple or white candle, and as you blow it out ask for love and light to surround your home and those you love.

PSYCHIC PROTECTION AT NIGHT

If you do feel especially anxious or afraid, or your children are having nightmares or night terrors, you can place yourself or your little ones in a huge, invisible pink or purple protective pavilion of crystal as you sleep. My own children sometimes choose a crystal to put under their pillow if they are afraid of sleeping alone or of the dark. The human psyche is remarkably fragile, and can be upset by internal as well as outside attack.

If you have a crystal wand, place it at the top of your bed with the receptive (rounded end) outwards, to absorb anything bad heading your way, and the creative end filling you with lovely clear energies to refresh you. Add a pink or purple stone so you aren't kept awake by all that energy pouring in. It's like recharging a battery overnight.

In the morning, either pour the negative energies from your crystals down the sink or into the earth. Or you can fashion them into a star and send them into the cosmos – you can do this through the train window if necessary.

The bedroom can be made harmonious by placing the four elements in the four main compass positions, a stone in the north for the earth and sound sleep, a fragrant pot-pourri in the east for a restful mind and abandonment of conscious thought, a mirror in the south for warmth and comfort, and water or a scented oil in the west for water and gentle dreams.

A bedtime spell

Light a soft green or pink candle for love and place it near the window. In its flame see the faces of those you love, and for a moment be close to them. You might get absent friends or family to light a candle at the same time each night and link in love. Blow out the candle and send loving light to every corner of the room to protect you while you sleep.

PSYCHIC SPRING CLEANING

Finally, witches of old always swept the ground they used for a magic circle with their broomstick. Had they lived in our own technological age, they would have used a hoover. A quick hoover round at the beginning or end of the day is a symbolic way of getting rid of any negative influences or unwanted emotional clutter. See the dark energies sucked away and replaced with pure white light. Your home is psychically clean.

MAGIC AND DIVINATION
IN THE HOME

T he wise woman of old did much of her magic at the wash tub. For this reason a whole range of ancient superstitions grew up around the wash tub and sink:

- If you wash up together you will have a happy marriage.
- It is unlucky to throw water away after sunset.
- After washing your hands first thing in the morning, don't shake the water off your hands or you'll disperse good luck.
- Sailors' wives should not wash up on the day a ship sails for fear of washing away the boat.
- If you dry your washing between showers your man will always love you.
- If you wash your hands in the same water as someone else you'll quarrel with them. The second person must make the sign of the cross in the water, or more rudely, spit into it.
- If you dry your hands on the same towel at the same time as another person, you'll go begging together.

Such old wives' tales were shared in communal wash or brewhouses, or at the river, as women scrubbed the clothes. Quite spontaneously, pictures or patterns would be seen in the water. The problem with conventional crystal balls is that the harder you stare into them the less you may see, because your expectations and anxieties are blocking the natural images that emerge from your mind's eye. An ovenware bowl, transparent or of smoked glass, filled with water, is very effective. You can put a candle or torch behind it to cast patterns on the water, and you can ripple the water with your fingers and see what patterns emerge. Simplest of all, however, is:

Washing-up bowl scrying

Put cold water into a bowl and squeeze a concentrated green liquid in drop by drop. It won't make bubbles, but will swirl round and round quite naturally in a series of shapes. You may want to ask it a question as you pour in the liquid, or allow the images to make up their own story. Change the water if you need to.

How do you know what the images mean? Trust yourself. The first interpretation that comes into your head is the correct one. Over time you will build up a whole symbol system that becomes remarkably similar to traditional interpretations of symbols.

- Judith, a TV presenter in her thirties, saw the image of a man, which she took to be a man on the other side of the world to whom she was attracted. The next image confirmed this, as it formed the kind of tree which grew where he lived.

Judith had that day booked a flight and three-week holiday to see him, although her career at home was at a turning point. The images confirmed the rightness of her decision, and when she did go, months later, she was offered work there as well.

To understand the situation further, Judith carried out:

A second washing-up divination, one specially linked to love, and based on an old Hallowe'en ritual

Put two corks, or traditionally acorns, in the bowl of water. If they instantly float close, a relationship will develop rapidly; if you are old marrieds, you are close to each other on a very deep level. If they float completely apart, maybe you have an unresolved worry you need to share, or are not ready for deep love yet. Go slowly. If they float close, then away and back again, that's a normal relationship – you may not touch the stars, but you'll be able to overcome the problems life throws at you.

Judith's corks floated in a strange way, the one following the other which did not pull away but floated slowly round as though on its everyday course. Judith interpreted this as meaning that she needed to follow her heart and go to her friend's world, since cross-world communication was not enough for her to be sure of a future.

There are many other forms of water scrying that can be practised at home.

Watch the suds and waterfalls formed by the washing machine in the local launderette, and let the images tell their watery story.

OILS

Drop dark-coloured bath oils, oil paint from an old tube, or ink, on to the surface of water. See what images appear. If you use either a medicine dropper or a very thin brush, you can watch an image build up and change. If you are careful you can add two or three colours and find that they form different areas of the same image.

HERBS

Because of their healing and magical properties, herbs are excellent for home-made divination. Use chopped dried herbs, freshly gathered if you have the time and inclination, or from the glass jars on sale commercially. Shake a handful of herbs on to a piece of kitchen paper. See the image formed and then gather the herbs together in the paper and toss it or swirl the herbs round to see what new patterns emerge.

Parsley, sage, rosemary and thyme are, as the ancient song says, traditional divinatory herbs, but you can use any that you have around the kitchen so long as the individual leaves are solid and separate, rather than powdery.

TEA AND COFFEE READINGS

Traditional readings of tea leaves can be refined by flattening a wet tea bag or individual coffee filter, the kind you are often served in cafés. Look at the shape formed behind the gauze.

However, you can use traditional tea leaves or coffee grounds. Don't worry about following complicated rituals, because you are using personal inner magic and can develop your own as and if you need it. Some traditionalists insist you swirl the leaves three times clockwise with your left hand before draining. There are so many variations, but they are all ways of performing a repetitive physical action so that your unconscious wisdom may come into operation.

Earl Grey tea is often recommended, but if you use your usual tea or brand of ground coffee, your personality is strongly etched on the process. Drain any remaining liquid off and see what picture or pattern the leaves form.

You can either think of a specific issue or question as you swirl, or allow the tea pictures to lead you. It may be helpful to swirl the leaves after the first picture to form a second or even third image, so you can build up a story as you would with a Tarot pack. If necessary add a little warm water to re-float the leaves between each image, if they seem to be sticking together rather than forming a clear image.

Tea-leaf reading works just as well with a paper cup and piece of blotting paper as the finest Crown Derby, so you can easily do a quick reading away from home.

Making your own symbol system

The idea of memorising a hundred or more tea-leaf symbols from a book can be very daunting and counter-productive. Learning by rote actually blocks natural intuitive processes and knowledge.

All divinatory symbols have common roots in the universal symbolism and mythology of mankind. For example, a butterfly symbolises to many people a transformation, a tree quiet persistence and strength, and a baby the beginnings of a new venture, especially in personal relationships. We begin to acquire and interpret images from early childhood, and by our teens and twenties all possess a powerful innate symbol system, built partly on what we have read, but also rooted in our own unique interpretation of the world.

The universal symbols in divination are mitigated by this personal world view, and if another person's images replace our own, we lose access to our own intuitive wisdom.

Another problem with traditional tea-leaf reading methods is that such systems are often given a fortune-telling bias. This can be misleading, and may set us along a wrong path, or worse still, leave us afraid to make our own decisions. However, images, interpreted intuitively, i.e. according to the spontaneous meaning that comes instantly, can be used far more creatively to reveal our real fears and feelings, which may be very different from those of which we were consciously aware. They can also suggest possible paths to success and happiness, based on the deep intuitive knowledge we all possess.

At first the symbols that appear may seem random. However, you'll find that the same images do appear time and time again in whatever form of divination you are using. You can build up a symbol notebook, and should find that you have around 50 constant images with perhaps ten or 20 minor variations. I've listed my main 50 symbols purely as an example, but you will probably find yours differ quite considerably. You might like to try mine as a trigger for your own. I can trace hints of the runes and Tarot in them, but many go back to the dreams of my childhood and the images I used to see in sand and in the glowing embers of the fire.

1. **An acorn** – a new plan that needs to be put into action now if it is to bear fruit later.

2. **An anchor** – putting obstacles in my own way to avoid moving into the unknown.

3. **An angel** – looking for a magical answer, rather than doing something about a problem.

4. **An ant** – success through hard work, involving step-by-step progress and perseverance.

5. **An arrow** – the need for swift, direct action towards a particular target.

6. **A baby** – a new beginning, whether at work or in a relationship.

7. **A bird** – the desire to escape either mentally or physically from a restricting situation.

8. **A book** – the need to follow the conventional path and pay attention to detail.

9. **A butterfly** – a complete change in direction after a crisis or loss.

10. **A castle** – material security is important at present.

11. **A chain or rope** – feeling trapped by circumstance or people, but needing to accept the restrictions now rather than waste energy resisting.

12. **A church** – the desire for approval from authority figures.

13. **Clouds** – temporary doubts that shouldn't stand in the way of change or progress.

14. **A coffin or gravestone** – not death, but time to move on to another phase.

15. **A coin** – knowing that there's a price to pay for change, but realising it's worth the risk.

16. **A crossroads** – needing to choose between two options rather than letting others make the choice.

17. **A dog** – the need to trust an old friend, or stick with an old relationship.

18. **A drum** – a lot of uproar from 'nearest and dearest' to mask a real problem or sneakiness.

19. **A duck** – following the natural course rather than swimming against the crowd.

20. **An eagle** – an issue that is very important and involves principles.

21. **An egg** – waiting for the right time for action.

22. **A *fish*** – needing to be adaptable and respond quickly to unexpected change.

23. **A *flag*** – the need to show solidarity with a friend or family member, even if you disagree with them.

24. **A *flower or flowers*** – develop potential friendships and be conciliatory in relationships and business.

25. **A *fox*** – treachery, beware of flatterers.

26. **A *horse*** – being strong and supportive to those around you.

27. **A *house*** – the practical organisation of life, needing to touch home base.

28. **A *king or crown*** – seeking success in the material world and asserting a separate identity.

29. **A *kite*** – trying to move too fast.

30. **The *moon*** – a desire to avoid harsh reality; taking the line of least resistance.

31. **A monkey** – the need to avoid direct confrontations and avoid offering commitments that can't be fulfilled.

32. **A nail** – the need to avoid hazards and obstacles, especially if the nail is sticking upwards.

33. **A necklace** – the likely success of a venture. If the necklace is broken, beware of leaving the task unfinished.

34. **A nun** – time to withdraw from life and the battles of others for a while, and rest more.

35. **An owl** – a decision is wise.

36. **An oyster or open shell** – look beyond the surface in a new, seemingly unpromising, relationship or offer.

37. **A purse** – sort out unresolved money issues.

38. **A queen** – taking care of the world and maybe overdosing on its problems (often appears prior to the image of the nun).

39. **A ring** – a promise of security that needs close examination, whether in relationships or work, as there are underlying doubts.

40. **A river** – going along with whatever is on offer for now, using the means to hand.

41. **A road** – the need to keep going, although it seems endless.

42. **A rose** – accepting love unconditionally.

43. **A snake or serpent** – being tempted to take a sneaky short-cut.

44. **A star** – wishing for an ideal solution and regretting missed opportunities.

45. **The sun** – hidden ambitions and talents not yet developed. Fulfilling potential, even in small ways.

46. **A sword** – the need to use logic to resolve an issue, and resist emotional blackmail.

47. **A tree** – the need to stand firm and persist, even if other people cast doubts on a project or relationship.

48. **An umbrella** – anticipate hazards and avoid them.

49. **A waterfall** – fear of taking a chance because there are no guarantees of security, but knowing the alternative is stagnation.

50. **A witch** – using inspiration rather than logic to solve a problem. Responding creatively, even to negativity.

How does the personal symbolism system work? Choose your preferred form of divination and make one, two or three images one after the other to develop a coherent picture. See how the images apply to your life. There are no right answers, only clues that are useful to your present situation.

A tea-leaf reading

- Beth wanted to buy a motorbike as it was ideal for commuting through heavy traffic, but her parents were worried about her safety and offered to buy her a small car if she abandoned the idea. Since Beth was training as a silversmith at college, and had only her grant to live on, the offer was very tempting. However, she felt it was important to escape the influence of her parents, though she could not afford to leave home. Beth used my symbolism as a basis and decided to read her tea leaves.

The first symbol she made was a bird, which suggested she wanted to escape from a restricting situation, so perhaps the motorbike was just a way of asserting that she did want to be separate from her parents. With the high cost of living, adult children often do remain in the family nest, and this can be stifling for both parents and children.

Beth's second image, made by swirling the leaves round again, was a waterfall, which she saw, like me, as taking a risk rather than risking stagnation. I suggested that meant that buying the motorbike was a good move, but Beth felt it referred to a suggestion made by a tutor, who had seen her work and suggested she went to Italy for a year. There was an exchange programme which would pay only living expenses, but would give Beth the opportunity to learn something of jewellery design, which was her real interest.

The third image was a door, which wasn't among the basic symbols I'd suggested, but Beth instantly interpreted as moving into another sphere and facing the unknown. She decided not to buy a motorbike straight away, but to explore the possibilities of spending a year in Italy.

Sometimes the question we ask isn't the issue we need answering, but our own divination can uncover the underlying trend and the path we could perhaps try or at least consider.

Your unique symbol

You may find that whatever form of divination you use, a particular symbol appears in a key position. This is your own unique symbol, that seems to represent not how the world sees you, but your inner core. This may be a symbol that has consistently appeared in dreams, visions and real life at significant moments, what Jung would call 'synchronicity' or a meaningful coincidence. You may find that this dominant image alters over time as you evolve. You may return to an earlier constant image in times of stress. By noting its appearance you can often tell when an issue is central to your being, and so worth fighting.

Alternative symbols

I mentioned that there are many minor symbols that may appear occasionally. If at first you note down all the symbols that appear and your 'off-the-top-of-your-head' interpretation, you can sort out those which appear regularly and ones that only crop up now and then. You may well find that the meanings evolve over time, and that you need to modify or even rewrite your list after a few months. Once you have a basic template, however, divination by scrying can address both your everyday questions and deeper issues of spirituality.

TOY-BOX SPELLS

Children have no problem using symbols. A toy car or plane can transport them anywhere. A doll or a teddy bear can become family or friend. My own children have an entire cuddly world ruled by a toy lion, complete with cuddly hospital, prison and even a cuddly church. The way to cuddly heaven is via the local rubbish tip, because that was where a giant lion, who lost his stuffing, was assigned.

Because children can graft magic on to anything, they have no problems making their dreams come true, if only for a while. Even today, with all the wealth of technology producing ever more expensive toys, a stick can be a sword, a piece of cloth a cherished friend, and stones and marbles the building blocks for whole worlds. What is more, playing in sand, mud and in woods is still far more exciting than simulated adventure worlds.

As adults, we have lost that early creativity. New Age shops and mail order catalogues sell expensive tools for doing magic that can actually take us away from the real power that resides just beyond the imagination we used so richly in childhood.

Magic, like childhood games, depends on using symbols to represent what we want. We then focus on that object and release our desires into the cosmos. The contents of any child's toy box provides all you need to do magic spells. If you have no children or toys from your own childhood, you could buy a set of small china ornaments or silver charms, or go to a car boot sale and buy a whole selection of toy cars, boats, tiny teddies, dolls and toy houses to keep in your magic box.

Crayons or felt-tip pens and coloured paper are ideal to draw a magic circle and allow you to use colours that reflect your wishes. (*See* the colour list in Chapter 1.)

A toy-box spell

Draw a circle in bright yellow, the colour of Mercury, for communication. Place a red dot, the colour of Mars, in the centre. A dot within a circle is the astrological sign for the sun, a symbol for making dreams happen.

The four elements

For earth, place a toy animal or toy gnome in the north of the circle, for air a toy plane in the east, for fire a toy fire engine in the south, and for water a toy boat in the west.

As you place each element symbol, concentrate on the properties of that element in making your dreams happen – the practical input of earth, the logic of air, the inspiration of fire and the versatility of water.

Draw a green cross bisecting the segments – the old astrological sign of the earth – to make the action in the real world.

Now for the symbol of your desire. If you want love, take a doll, for friendship a tiny teddy, for travel, a toy car, plane, train or boat, and a flag or postcard for where you want to go. Some toy coins represent money, and for a house move, a small house or some Lego bricks. Pass the items clockwise through the elements, seeing the power of each giving reality to your dream. Place the object on the red dot in the centre.

Now shine a mirror on to the ceiling above the circle; as you do so, see your wish fly like a sunbeam to join the cosmos.

Go out and do something totally childlike, and leave behind the heaviness of adult reality.

TOOL BOX DIVINATION AND SPELLS

The contents of the tool box or garden shed, or metal ornaments and trinkets around the house are a powerful focus for one of the oldest forms of magic.

Metal was in early times and in all cultures, from China to Ancient Egypt, mined according to certain ancient and traditional magical rituals.

Alchemy was the forerunner of modern chemistry, medicine and metallurgy, and was practised extensively in the Middle Ages in Western Europe. Its aim was to turn base metals into gold by a process somewhere between magic and science. The underlying aim was to find the philosopher's stone that could cause this miraculous transformation. Chinese alchemy concentrated on finding an elixir to give eternal life.

The Ancient Egyptians worked with alloys, and the Father of western alchemy was a semi-mythical half-god, Hermes Trismegistus, a form of the Egyptian and Greek gods of magic and wisdom, Thoth and Hermes.

The Ancient Egyptians developed the idea that the world was formed out of a chaotic mass called *prima materia*, by divine force. In western alchemy it was believed that all things could be reduced back to this first matter through dissolving and combining to create a new substance. King Sol, sulphur, the sun, the fiery principle, Queen Luna, the moon, and mercury, the watery principle, combined to create a divine son who was symbolic of the elusive philosopher's stone. Later salt was added for the earth, as an element necessary to support life.

The Arabs developed these ideas, which spread to Western Europe through Spain in the twelfth century. Alchemy remained at a height until Tudor times. John Dee, a famous alchemist, was astrologer and physician to Elizabeth I. Astrology and the influence of the heavenly spheres were central to their beliefs. 'As above, so below,' was the alchemists' maxim. Alchemists would work hour after hour following complex rituals with little success, although they learned a great deal that contributed to modern chemistry and healing. However, it was said that one alchemist Nicholas Flamel, in the fourteenth century, did transmute mercury into silver or gold three times.

Alchemists based their study on dreams and visions, with fabulous animals – the snake who swallowed his own tail, the phoenix who rose from the ashes, the salamander, the lengendary fire lizard, and the pelican who fed her young from the blood of her own breast. These creatures symbolised chemical and mystical principles that to the alchemists were one and the same.

Although alchemy was finally discredited in the early nineteenth century, with the discovery of oxygen and the composition of water, much of its wisdom is being re-discovered as having scientific validity. For example, Paracelsus discovered chemical compounds in the early sixteenth century, and found that wounds would heal naturally if kept clean and dry, a revolutionary concept at the time.

From these early traditions, metals became symbolically associated with different planets, and so represent different magical powers.

METAL DIVINATION

Even today metal magic is a powerful form of divination. All you need is an assortment of nuts and bolts, whatever you like from your local hardware store in aluminium, brass, copper, iron, steel, tin and lead, as long as they are of a standard size and shape and so can be put into a bag to pick at random.

If you have a lot of old jewellery you may have a plain silver, copper, gold or pewter ring, and you can get rings of other metals from a hardware store. Or you may be able to form a collection of old coins in different metals. I buy a lot of ancient coins in different metals very cheaply from a local museum. Industrial museums are especially good sources. Or you can use flat plain discs from the hardware shop. You can mix these with coins of similar sizes, or go to a mineral shop and buy small rocks containing the metals. Junk shops with baskets of assorted trinkets are often a good source for small metal objects or rings.

Find seven different forms to represent the seven major heavenly bodies.

If you can't get a particular metal you can paint a stone of the right shape and size in metallic paint, or even paint circular cardboard or wood discs with each of the appropriate paints. Use grey pewter colour paint for lead.

Metal meanings

The sun – brass, gold or a gold alloy represents the conscious achievement side of our nature, and says it's time to develop our abilities and to succeed in whatever way makes us feel fulfilled. Take an assertive but creative approach. However, beware you don't ride roughshod over others in your enthusiasm.

Gold is also sacred to the Northern solar goddess, Sol, and to Balder, the Norse solar deity of the growing light.

The moon – silver or a silvery alloy stands for the unconscious wisdom that comes through our dreams, visions and sudden insights. Find an unlikely solution – it will be the right one. But beware the easy path.

Silver is also sacred to Ostara, Northern goddess of spring, who is Mani, the moon goddess.

Mercury – use aluminium for an interactive approach to any problems. Clear communication both with yourself and the outside world is vital. Don't be tempted to be sneaky. The other metal of this planet, quicksilver or mercury, is rarely used because of its dangers. Mercury is also sacred to Odin, the All-Father of the Norse tradition and to Woden of the Anglo-Saxons.

Venus – use copper or lodestone in all relationship issues, and be aware of the underlying meaning and intent rather than the actual words. Don't resort to emotional blackmail, and remember that Venus as the evening rather than the morning star is not all sweetness and light. Copper is also sacred to Frigg, the wife of Odin, and mother goddess of women and fertility.

Mars – use iron or steel to stand up for what you believe is right, and be prepared to go against the crowd. Don't repress negative feelings or off-load them on to others. Iron is also sacred to the Northern Tyr, the defender god, with his magical iron sword.

Jupiter – use tin or bronze for conventional wisdom, and following all the necessary steps to success, rather than relying on intuitive leaps. While idealism and principles are vital, avoid being totally uncompromising over less important issues.

Tin is also sacred to Thor, who was said to have discovered the metal as it ran from stones that had been heated. This legend was later transferred to the Christian St Piran of Cornwall, formerly a great area of tin mining in Britain.

Saturn – use lead or pewter for the ability to see when it's time to move on; see any restrictions in your path as an opportunity for positive change and an alternative approach or perspective. Avoid pessimism and the belief that you can't control events.

Lead is also sacred to Seater and the Norse trickster, Loki, in its less positive aspects.

How to use simple metal divination

Take a plain scarf or cloth about a foot square, and mark it with three circles, each one inside the other. The innermost circle represents the inner you and things close to the heart. Survival issues will be reflected here. Draw round a saucer for this circle.

The middle circle, drawn round a teaplate placed over the inner circle, represents your mind, your hopes, fears, feelings and dreams.

The outer circle, drawn round a dinner plate placed over the inner circles, represents the outer world of action and the everyday world.

The area outside the circle represents an area where things are not moving, perhaps because of your own fears, or perhaps because others are blocking your progress.

You can draw the circles in indelible marker.

Take three pieces of metal from your selection without looking as you choose, and throw them on to the cloth. Interpret the message according to where the pieces of metal land on the cloth.

If you have read *Runes, Moon or Crystal Divination for Today's Woman* (Foulsham), you will be familiar with this very simple but powerful form of divination.

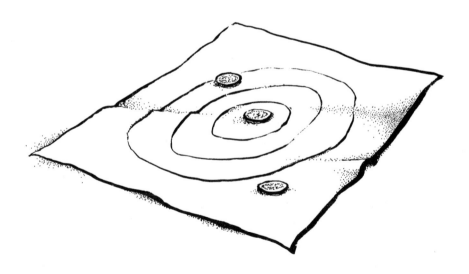

Kate's metal divination

- Kate's job at a radio station is under threat and she is uncertain whether to wait until the last moment in the hope of a buy-out of the firm or whether to take a job she has been offered in a PR firm, a job she does not really want, but which would offer security.

Kate uses a collection of coins in different metals. She throws:

1. Jupiter (tin) in her innermost circle. This suggests that in her heart of hearts she is not ready to take a chance, and since she has a large mortgage should perhaps opt for security rather than job satisfaction.

2. Saturn (pewter) in her middle circle. This implies that Kate is letting her doubts and regrets run round and round in her mind, and that she should talk about them to resolve her feelings.

3. The sun (gold) outside the circles may mean that Kate is seeing the situation as an either/or. There may be other job opportunities in her own field, but her regrets and fears for the future are preventing her from using her natural initiative.

On the spur of the moment, Kate phones a top radio station that is opening, and is offered a test. She is hopeful of getting a job in some capacity, and working her way up if necessary.

If, in a cast of three, you read the metals in the order you throw them, you may see a developing story or idea.

Daily metal divination – choose a different metal each morning or at decision times

Place your metal items in a bag. Pull out one when you've got to make a decision, or first thing in the morning; it will guide you to a possible course of action, as well as pointing out the pitfalls. You may find that you choose the same metal several days in a row, in which case you know that is an area that needs action.

Carry your chosen metal round with you all day to reflect the quality of that particular deity. If you do make a collection of rings – not forgetting the hardware store as well as jewellers and antique shops as sources – you can pick one without looking each morning, and wear it on your finger or on a chain round your neck during the day, or sleep with it at night. We tend to wear gold or silver rings, but sometimes an aluminium ring can help us communicate with ourselves, or a pewter one remind us that we shouldn't be deterred by obstacles.

Metal spells

If you look around your home you will find examples of the seven basic metals. I found an imitation brass disc for the sun, a silver locket for the moon, some aluminium foil for Mercury, an iron horseshoe for Mars, a copper bracelet for Venus, a tin coin for Jupiter, and a battered pewter tankard for Saturn.

A metal spell for standing up for yourself if your boss or family criticise you or make you feel inadequate

Use either an aluminium foil dish or piece of foil for the clear communication of Mercury. Put crossed stainless steel knives of Mars inside for cutting through the fear of speaking out, and to cut the tangle of frustration. Finally, place some gold foil circles for the positive energy and confidence of the sun inside the foil or foil dish.

Shake silver glitter or silver sequins for the unconscious power of the moon over the knives and the gold discs; as you do so, shake out all your anger and negativity and replace it with positive energy and belief in your own worth.

Uncross the knives and put them side by side to symbolise the new equality in the relationship, and leave your dish or piece of silver foil where it can catch both the sunlight and the moonlight. Leave it in a place for a full month while you put your new determination into practice. Add more glitter if your resolve weakens.

METAL AND ASTROLOGY

Each metal is also ruled by an astrological sign that, with its planet, provides the key to its most effective use in spells.

Aries – 21 March–20 April: Iron Ruled by Pluto. (Read as Mars, its old ruler.) The iron of Aries can galvanise you into change and make you stand up to bullies.

Taurus – 21 April–21 May: Copper Ruled by Venus. The copper of Taurus can help you through difficult patches in relationships, whether at work or home, rather than you giving up.

Gemini – 22 May–21 June: Chrome Ruled by Mercury. The chrome of Gemini can enable you to adapt your ideas to reach a compromise, when confrontation would be destructive.

Cancer – 22 June–22 July: Silver Ruled by the moon. The silver of Cancer can help you to reach the heart of any situation, with sensitivity.

Leo – 23 July–23 August: Gold Ruled by the sun. The gold of Leo will provide you with the courage of your convictions.

Virgo – 24 August–23 September: Nickel Ruled by Mercury. The nickel of Virgo will ensure you don't cut corners or settle for second best.

Libra – 24 September–23 October: Bronze Ruled by Venus. The bronze of Venus will enable you to be fair-minded, even to those who oppose you.

Scorpio – 24 October–22 November: Steel Ruled by Pluto. (Read as Mars, its old ruler.) The steel of Scorpio will help you believe in yourself when others cast doubts.

Sagittarius – 23 November–21 December: Brass Ruled by Jupiter. The brass of Sagittarius will ease you into new avenues and encourage you to try new ideas.

Capricorn – 22 December–20 January: Pewter Ruled by Saturn. The pewter of Capricorn will prevent you from being diverted from your goal.

Aquarius – 21 January–19 February: Aluminium Ruled by Uranus. (Read as Mercury, its ancient ruler.) The aluminium of Aquarius assures you that being alone isn't the same as being lonely.

Pisces – 20 February–20 March: Tin Ruled by Uranus. (Read as Jupiter, its ancient ruler.) The tin of Pisces enables you to transform set-backs into positive experiences.

If you can't get any of these metals use an alloy substitute or one of similar colour, or even a metallic paint or foil as you did for divination. You can use your zodiacal metal, which is also linked with your ruling planet, to galvanise your energies. You may wish to add the metal of the sign and planet that reflects your current need, or is that of the person involved.

Other metals ruled by the same planet as your own sign can also strengthen your resolve. You can use any forms of the metal – rings, discs, tiny pieces, small objects, or your nuts and bolts. Any mixture will do. The objects don't even have to be the same size or shape. Any cutlery, scissors or tools will be fine. If you do your spell on aluminium foil you can be sure your spell will reaffirm your own identity and unique qualities. You can use any of the metallic foils available from art shops to add the particular quality of that colour or metal. Indeed, some people do all their metal magic with different kinds of foil.

An astrological metal spell

- Christine has been in a wheelchair since she was very young, and runs a very successful detective agency. She wanted to expand her business into security, and was offered a loan by her bank. She needed to live over her new premises, which would involve adapting them considerably. However, this would be far cheaper and more convenient than maintaining her separate living accommodation, which was several miles away, and she could get a grant for part of the work. Her only problem was with the insurers, who saw her incapacity as a fire and security risk in the evenings when she was upstairs alone. How could she do what she wanted, and yet get the necessary cover to begin operations?

Her birth sign is Scorpio and her metal steel, so Christine had a basic belief that the course was the right one for her, though the problems with getting insurance had caused her doubts. She also had the ancient god of war, Mars, rooting for her.

What Christine needed was to transform her difficulties into positive assets, so she used tin, the metal of Pisces. She had some old tin coins, also a symbol of her prospective financial success. She used a stainless steel knife to emphasise her determination to cut through problems and the need to use logic.

She found some gold-coloured foil and cut a golden disc to give her the power of the sun and the energy to realise her dream. She put her four coins at the four main compass points – north, south, east and west – and the knife pointing to the east, the spring position, for a new beginning. As she placed the knife on each coin in turn she visualised a gleaming steel blade slicing through the difficulties, and the tin not as a separate coin, but as a vast sheet bending and adapting to build her a shining ramp upstairs to her living quarters, strengthened by the wind of the east, the sun of the south, the rain of the west and the snow of the north.

Christine knew a conventional ramp wouldn't work as the building had exceptionally high ceilings and the wide, winding stairs weren't suitable to fit a lift. She took the knife and used it to cut an apple into four. She saw the apple as representing the fruits of her efforts. The apple is also the tree of Taurus, the sign of patience and endurance in the face of difficulty, and in her case, her disability. As I said, you can borrow the qualities of other signs. She placed each segment on one of the coins as a symbol of her efforts bearing fruit, and then turned the disc so the positions were reversed. Could she live downstairs? Then how could she get upstairs alone?

Christine lit an indigo candle for her zodiacal sign and a white candle for the Piscean power of adaptability. She passed the knife through the flame to give it the power of fire, and placed it horizontally for the upstairs, then placed the coins into a path below. As she held the candle over each coin, wax dripped on to the foil between the knife and coin, making a third level. In her mind she saw the tin being moulded into a shape, a sloping mezzanine floor linking the two levels. The answer was simple. She could live downstairs during the part of the day when she would be alone, and the office would be on the mezzanine floor, as the ceilings were very high, and linked with the upstairs by a gently sloping ramp. Upstairs would be a showroom for home security devices, which would open only when she had staff for it.

The insurance company was happy with the plans and 'Top to Bottom Security' opened its doors.

IRON MAGIC

In early times iron which was cut from meteorites was seen as a gift from the gods. Early man believed it was magic from heaven, and proof against witches and evil spirits. Horseshoes were believed to keep a home safe; they traditionally point upwards, so luck would not run out. As the metal of Mars, iron was seen as a symbol of strength and was often used in banishing magic.

Traditionally it was believed that if a person had toothache they should rub the afflicted gum with a new nail until it bled. The nail was then hammered into an oak tree, which would take away the pain.

This technique can be used to get rid of negativity, anger or resentment. Choose a nail to represent something you are angry about, and hammer it into a small piece of oak wood. Either burn the wood and bury the charred nail, or use the wood as a marker for new plants.

MAGIC IN THE
GARDEN AND PARK

E very culture has a wonderful legendary garden, with abundant fruit, trees, and animals and a Tree of Life, granting immortality and health to its inhabitants.

The Greeks borrowed the word 'paradise' from the Persians, who used it to describe enclosed and extensive pleasure grounds of the Persian kings. There was a popular medieval belief that earthly paradise was an island or land where everything was beautiful and death and decay unknown.

Gardens and parks, nature contained within limits, have retained their magical associations. The smallest back yard, a suburban garden or local recreation ground can provide a natural focus for and amplification of our own inner powers. When I was working in Bristol, I discovered an ordinary park behind a housing estate that contained not only unspoiled woodland and a winding stream, but its own wishing well.

The garden, the local park or even a window box are rich sources of magic. Tree, herb and flower magic goes back to the older, slower time before people lived in towns and barely looked up to see the sky. But the magic is still there, and can be used for spells and divination.

Because the world is so noisy, it is easy to miss the sounds of nature – running water, birdsong, the wind in the trees. If we listen, these natural oracles will answer the questions that go round and round in our heads.

GETTING IN TOUCH WITH THE
NATURAL ELEMENTS IN YOUR GARDEN

Earth

Stand barefoot in your garden as the sun rises. Hold a dark brown pebble, or if you collect crystals, a smoky brown quartz, dark brown streaked fossilised wood or brown jasper. Circle your crystal clockwise around your frame, feeling each bone, muscle and sinew warmed and renewed by the symbolic strength of the earth. You are symbolically marking out your self, a self that has unique beauty and worth. Feel the sun warming your body and your own root energies rising from acceptance to the desire to bring your dreams to fruition. This desire will eventually link to the next area of inner power.

Go for an early morning walk, whether around streets, to a park or in the countryside, and do not worry about direction, commitments or timetables. Let your feet guide you and your mind. Do not mull over problems, unfinished chores or assignments, but accept whatever impressions enter your consciousness through your five senses; an early morning bread shop, a scented bush in a front garden, the hum of distant traffic, birdsong, colours, whether from hoardings or the natural paintbox of experience. Taste the salt if you are near the sea, or garlic wafting from a delicatessen.

You may momentarily link with older images, a plough drawn by huge brown oxen, clogs sparking outside a disused factory, fragrances of spices from an abandoned warehouse, gulls which flew over ships setting out on perilous voyages. These are just a few of the pictures evoked by my own wanderings. Early morning is a good time for your imagination to link with the impressions left by that past, and such interdimensional fantasies can put the present world into perspective.

Bring back a stone or pebble and place it in your garden, whether as the beginning of a small circle of your own, or edging a path. Let it symbolise the first step towards an endeavour, and each time you make a new step add to a stone circle, path or even cairn. Plant herbs or flowers that will bloom golden or brown, St John's wort, herb of midsummer, pansies, wallflowers or marigolds.

Air

Air represents power all round you, especially on a windy day. Stand in your garden or a park and hear the wind speak. Climb to the top of a hill, open your arms wide and shout out your current mantra, 'I exist', 'I am free', 'I will succeed', over and over again as you run down the hill as fast as you can.

Cycling can also focus air power. Whether you are an experienced cyclist with a 24-gear mountain bike, or like me, ride a sedate adult tricycle, you can coil your body as you cycle up a steep hill, feeling your elbows and ankles curved inwards, each knot of your spine bearing down as you again draw in your intent as a single word or phrase, spoken out loud or within your mind.

When you reach the top of the hill, pause momentarily and feel the power pulsating within you, and see your aim as a gift wrapped up in string, loosely knotted so you just need to pull the first piece for it to uncoil and open. Then freewheel down the hill, letting the rushing wind and blurring backdrop carry your triumphant mantra to the skies.

Buy a children's bubble blower and fill a container with thick, soapy liquid. Visualise whatever it is you want or hope to achieve, and blow a circle of bubbles, higher and higher, all the time seeing your ambitions come true.

Finally blow a single bubble larger and larger, very slowly so as not to break it. Feel the mirrored power of your inner bubble getting stronger and wider. Gently release the bubble and watch your own confidence rise sky high.

Fire

The sun, or a mirror reflecting light beams, can be your fire.

Even today, some people swear by weather magic and carry out spells to make it rain or make the sun shine. The old spells reflect the power we all have to make our inner sun shine, amplified by the natural power of fire magic.

On a sunny day, catch the reflection of the sun in your garden pond or a bucket of water. Now gently drop in a golden coloured coin – a pound coin will do – or a gold ring, and watch the light beams spread. Feel your own inner fire expanding, and all the possibilities awakening.

Say your mantra of power or success, and when you feel the warmth touch every fibre of your being, impose your own reflection in front of the sun so it becomes a halo.

If you have used a bucket don't throw the water away when you've finished. Use it for making petal perfume from a fragrant golden rose. If you have a pond, buy a pair of glinting goldfish to keep the gold within.

You can also use a pot of marigolds, a sunflower or any other golden flower to amplify your inner sun. Place it in the centre of your window or the garden and use its golden essence to spread sunshine over your garden or back yard. Concentrate on each petal; see them shedding a golden aura like a sunbeam, with the sunbeams spiralling together into a golden ray of sunlight. When you no longer need the sunshine, separate it out into individual sunbeams to return it to the petals. Thank the flower and give it extra plant food or a warm sheltered corner in which to grow.

Water

Garden ponds, pools in parks, even the local swimming pool when it first opens in the morning, offer accessible sources of water for magic, not forgetting the greatest and most untamed source of all, the sea, whose primitive power even pollution has not destroyed.

Go to a swimming pool in the early morning or evening, when there are few people to disturb your concentration. Choose a time when natural sunlight filters on to the water or coloured lights cast rainbows on the surface. If you are a confident swimmer, go down and coil yourself beneath the water while visualising your goal or the particular step you need to take. As you coil tighter and tighter, use a single word or phrase repeated in your head as a mantra, letting the word crescendo in your mind. When you feel ready to surface, push up hard, throwing out your arms or keeping your body like an arrow as you uncoil.

Although I am in my mid-forties and able to swim, I am still what my children call a 'goldfish swimmer', going round and round the edges of the pool, still finding it unnerving to go beyond my depth. I push my elbows and knees in close and crouch so that only my head is above the water, and repeat the same ritual, sometimes bobbing up and down in a rhythm with my youngest child, until I feel renewed enthusiasm and vigour, like an engine warmed up for action.

Move or swim slowly through water to re-absorb the power; then float, like a charged battery, powerful but calm.

A PSYCHIC DIET

It does not matter what shape and size we are so long as we are fit and feel happy with ourselves. However, the point may come when we start to feel unhealthy and out of sorts, usually because we have been snacking on unhealthy foods. Food and eating naturally belong to the earth realm of our life. When food moves out of the hunger/pleasure category into the air segment, i.e. as a way of stilling negative thoughts in the water realm, then we need to restore the elemental balance.

Your garden is the perfect place to work on your psychic diet. Take a symbol of what it is you want to give up, a small jar of jam or a chocolate biscuit, and dig a small hole to bury it. On top, plant fast-growing stocks or herbs, as a symbol of your new direction. We need to replace anything we give up so that the old habits don't return to fill a vacuum. Whenever you are tempted to eat snack foods for the wrong reason – pleasure is a right reason, boredom and depression aren't – go out to your garden and water your 'diet patch' before you give way to the temptation.

If you are still craving, bury the offending food and plant some more seeds. Of course it is wasteful to bury a cream bun, but at least it will feed the insects or decompose and nourish the soil. Inside you, it is wasted anyway.

Plant some seeds in your new patch, and if you still want something nice to eat, go out and choose a single item that will give you sensual pleasure. On the other hand, by the time you have walked to the corner shop, you may decide not to bother. If so, save the money you would have spent towards a treat (not necessarily food), when you are next feeling miserable.

ELEMENT SPELLS AND DIVINATION
IN THE PARK OR GARDEN

Earth scrying

Earth is the elemental realm inhabited by gnomes, who aren't a bit like the Disney characters in *Snow White*. If you're lucky enough to spot one in your garden or local park, he is more serious and likely to be offering practical insights rather than pouring treasures upon us.

The earth symbol is a pentacle, so you might like to use a coin as your focus. Keep it with you as a reminder that all things pass, and that today's life-and-death crisis will scarcely be remembered tomorrow.

Look for pictures in sand washed by the tide or on a river-bank, or where tyre tracks have passed through deep mud and dried. Ancient Egyptians used to interpret the cracks in earth baked by the sun. Allow a picture to come into your mind and interpret the image in your own way. It may offer an answer to something that is troubling you.

Earth divination

Take two or three rosebuds of the same size and at the same stage of development from a bush. If you wish, you can use different colours from adjoining bushes, or buy some at a florist's. Roses have been considered magical from earliest times.

The Greek god of silence stumbled upon Venus while she was entertaining a lover. Cupid, the son of Venus, bribed the god, with a white rose surrounded by white rosebuds, not to reveal what he had seen. From that day the white rose became a symbol of silence or secrecy. The Latin expression *sub rosa*, 'under the rose', means you are sworn to silence. The white rose was carved into doorways and above arches in banqueting rooms to remind guests that what they heard under the influence of liquid hospitality was to be kept secret. White roses are often placed near confessional booths in Catholic churches, and you'll usually find an engraved rose nearby.

Originally all roses were believed to have been white. Cupid was stung by a bee while admiring a rose, and became so angry he shot an arrow at the rose bush, causing it to bleed. The blooms turned red and thorns were created. However, another legend says roses became red when Cupid spilled wine over them.

Place the roses in water in separate vases. If you are considering a simple 'Either'/'Or', use two roses and designate one 'Yes' and the other 'No'. If the issue is more complex, you can use three roses or even more. The first rose to bloom fully gives you the answer.

• Annette, in her early twenties, did not know whether to settle with her boyfriend Tim whom she had known for years, or take an opportunity to stay with a relation in Canada for a year and earn her keep by working in their tourist hotel near Quebec. Her boyfriend was pressurising her to settle down, and her mother was also eager for her to settle with Tim, although Annette had not managed to get a job since leaving college. Tim could afford to keep them both.

Annette placed a red rose for marriage in one vase and a white rose for travel in a second. She felt there wasn't a third option, since Tim would neither come with her nor agree to wait.

After two days the red rose died, although it was well watered and had looked healthy. Annette felt that it symbolised her own feelings, that she would die inside if she settled for the safe option as a housewife. She realised that her relationship with Tim was a habit for both of them, and that if she did not travel now she would always regret it.

Tim and her mother were very angry, but Annette is determined to go to Canada in the autumn.

Air scrying

The air is inhabited by the sylphs. Maidens who played the field but always said 'No', are traditionally said to be transformed after death into sylphs. Sylphs sometimes appear as butterflies, telling you to value what you have today and not insist on guarantees or 'for evers'. The symbol is a sword; you can use a small paper knife or screwdriver, needles, pins, nails, screws or sharp tools to represent this element.

Look for pictures in the clouds, especially at sunrise and sunset or when they are moving fast. The wind swirling the leaves or even litter can make pictures across the air.

A very simple method of air divination is to write the two alternatives, or even 'Yes'/'No' to what you want to know, on two pieces of paper and drop them from an upper window into the garden. Get a child or trusted friend to tell you which answer lands first, unless you are a fast runner down stairs.

Another divinatory air method is to light a stick of incense – maybe jasmine for the intuitions of the moon, or sandalwood, a divinatory essence of the sun – in a sheltered corner of your garden or on the patio. Watch the gentle breeze lift the smoke, and read shapes formed by the smoke; if in doubt, put an old enamel plate behind and read the smoke marks left. Crumble the ash and you've got the added dimension of earth divination.

EARTH

WATER

AIR

FIRE

• Lesley has just retired and has discovered that she has a form of arthritis that will severely limit her mobility within a few years. She has always wanted to follow the Silk Road to Samarkand and then go on to stay in Tibet for a month. Now she wonders whether she should save her retirement nest egg to help her when her physical strength weakens. Lesley feels that with all the underlying emotions she would like to use the logic of air.

She goes to the top of a hill in her local park as the sun is setting. It is very windy and the clouds are moving fast. She sees a chariot and mountains, and above all a bent old monk in the clouds. She interprets the chariot as meaning movement and travel, taking her to see the places she wants to visit, because she knows that, though she can and will travel in times to come, she won't have the freedom she has now. She doesn't understand the significance of the old monk, though she knows there are many monasteries in Tibet.

To confirm her interpretation she picks up two feathers she finds, a white one from a pigeon and a black one from a crow. She decides that white is for 'Go' and black for 'Stay'. The two feathers are of very similar size and weight. The one that flies the highest will be the answer. The joy of DIY magic is that you make the rules, and as long as you set them in advance it can't fail. The black feather would not flutter, although later when Lesley tests it in her garden she finds it does fly. However, the white feather lifts in the breeze and is carried away.

Most magic such as this does seem to work once you've set the rules for the cosmic teams. People argue that it's the wind direction, but I've demonstrated the technique lots of times and the results always differ wildly and are invariably the best choice for the person concerned.

Lesley went to Tibet, where she met an old monk so bent with age he almost touched the ground. But he had the most wonderful hands, and held them over her and promised her that her illness would not develop. So far she has had far fewer symptoms. She feels he is her monk in the clouds.

Fire scrying

This is the realm of the legendary salamander or fire lizard. Its symbol is the magic wand, so any piece of twig, especially from a hazel tree, or a small piece of quartz crystal, will do as a focus. The salamander reminds us that all things are possible given imagination and courage to walk through the fire.

Light a bonfire in the garden, watch the sparks and embers making pictures – many of us did this as small children – and access all kinds of wonderful realms. Barbecue coals, too, can glow with patterns; you may find your favourite symbol among the steaks and sausages.

Light two candles, tapers or even incense cones in a sheltered spot in the garden. You can do this indoors, but you lose the effects of the patterns and pictures carried upwards in the smoke. Use each to represent an alternative choice. See which burns or goes out first, and the one that remains will give you the answer. This works for me, but you may wish to reverse the significance so the first to go out gives the answer. So long as you decide in advance the magic will work. If both candles go out at the same time, you'll know the questions need rephrasing.

- Suzy wants to be able to drive, but in spite of numerous lessons from friends as well as professionals, she cannot pass her test. Her brother has told her about an intensive 'learn and drive' holiday, but her last tutor told her she simply didn't have the aptitude and should stop wasting her money.

However, Suzy has the opportunity to move from an office job with a farming equipment manufacturer into sales, which will involve travelling to remote smallholdings and outlying farms, *if* she can drive.

She decides to scry for the answer, and lights two candles in her back yard, a golden-brown one for persisting and a grey one for giving up. Brown is the colour of a step-by-step earth approach, and grey talks of ending a phase, but she could have used any colour to represent her choice (*see* candle magic spells and a full list of candle colour meanings in Chapter 9).

Suzy says the candle which remains burning will give her the answer. The grey candle burns away first, though they were the same size and the brown candle was lit first.

However, she wants confirmation, and so looks at the shapes formed by the brown candle as it continues to burn – the shape of a car, an enclosure and animals, the farm. Since Suzy knows she can only take the job if she has a car, she makes one last attempt to learn to drive on the residential course, and succeeds.

Water scrying

Water is ruled by the undines, mythical water creatures. Undine herself was an elemental spirit who gained a soul by marrying a mortal and having a child, but paid the penalties of mortality.

I spoke about water scrying in Chapter 3 and suggested that cookware containers filled with water, or even a washing-up bowl and liquid, are ideal media. Water scrying is one that seems to come naturally to women.

If it's a question of deciding between two options, play psychic 'Pooh sticks' in a park where there is a narrow stream. Remember how Christopher Robin and Winnie-the-Pooh threw sticks into the water from a bridge and dashed to the other side to see which emerged first. All those obstacles and unpredictable eddies and swirls in the water prevent any stacking of the odds, so pick your two sticks, decide which one represents which option, and throw them off the upstream side of a bridge over a narrow stream or river. If someone else is involved, get them to throw one of the options. Cross to the downstream side of the bridge to see which one emerges first.

You can also use a piece of wood or toy yachts on a pond and float them across the water to see which reaches the other side first.

- Lily's choice centred on going to college at the age of 50 to take a degree in law, her youthful ambition that had been interrupted by pregnancy while she was still at school, marriage and a family before she was 20. She had brought the children up single-handed after her husband walked out; they were now grown-up and had left home. However, Lily had met Bob, a widower who wanted to marry her. Since he was much older he was taking early retirement, and wanted them to move to a place in the sun. He felt it would be a waste of time for Lily to take a degree, and that it would blight the years he hoped they would spend getting to know each other and enjoying life in a new country. Lily loved Bob, but felt she had already sacrificed her ambitions once.

  Lily went to the stream in her local park and carved 'College' on one stick and 'Bob' on the other. She threw them off the bridge and watched as her 'College' stick got tangled in the weeds while the 'Bob' stick sailed merrily on. She was disappointed, and I said she didn't have to abide by the decision. It was her choice. So she tried again, this time taking her

grandchildren to the boating lake and letting them have a toy yacht race. The boat she designated 'Bob' again came home by a good lead.

Still Lily insisted that she wanted college rather than Bob, however, and so we discussed if she could have both – she said no, as they were going to a part of Spain away from the normal retirement areas, where there was no English spoken and the nearest town was a hundred miles away.

Lily tried again. This time she went back to scrying with household objects, dropping ink from her fountain pen into a bowl of water. The ink made waves, which I said could be disrupting the retirement plans, but which she saw as the coast near where they would live. The second made a bed, and Lily smiled. No, it wasn't the marital bed, but the bed and breakfast Bob wanted to open for holidaymakers who wanted to get off the tourist track. The third drop made a palm tree; there were palm trees along the coastline.

Lily said it was uncanny, because deep in her heart she really wanted to go with Bob but felt she was betraying her early dream. We talked about how dreams might change over the years, and how fulfilment didn't necessarily mean ambition or 'going it alone', an idea as stereotyped as retiring to the sun with the man of her dreams. It sounded a lively retirement, and Lily said she had bought some Spanish language tapes though she hadn't intended on going. The water divination gave Lily permission to do what she really wanted and not what she thought she ought to do.

At home, you can use the garden pond or even fill a bowl of water. Make paper boats with the options written on and see which sinks first – the sinking ship I would say is the 'No' option.

HERB, FLOWER AND TREE MAGIC

Herb magic was one of the earliest forms of magical practice, and even today herbal medicine has many healing properties that modern pharmaceutics scarcely understands. Flowers, too, form a whole language, while trees were used in one of the early Druid and Celtic forms of divination, the ogham staves as well as the runes.

Natural astrology

For spells, the most effective form of magic links these natural substances with different zodiacal signs. I've drawn up a table of each sign so that you can use the relevant herb, flower and tree as your personal magical symbols to be used and kept around at times when you need special natural energies.

You may find that the natural substances of other zodiacal signs will help you when you need their particular qualities in your life. They are said to be at their most powerful during their zodiacal period. Try adding your own zodiacal herb or flower to any such spell, to make the issue integrate with your whole life.

Natural astrology is often neglected in favour of the more formal, predictive kind. By seeing astrology in terms of the natural world, however, we can regain the fluidity of early astrology and retain control over our own destiny.

Aries – 21 March–20 April
Herb – mustard
Flower – honeysuckle
Tree – hawthorn

These are natural substances of action and assertiveness, and so can be used by anyone who needs to stand out against injustice or make a radical change.

Taurus – 21 April–21 May
Herb – sorrel
Flower – rose
Tree – apple

These are natural substances of patience and fidelity, and so may be helpful to anyone in a difficult situation with no opportunity to walk away.

Gemini – 22 May–21 June
Herb – marjoram
Flower – lily of the valley
Tree – hazel

These are natural substances of adaptability and communication, and so offer these qualities to all who are trying to overcome obstacles.

Cancer – 22 June–22 July
Herb – tarragon
Flower – convolvulus
Tree – willow

These are natural substances to protect those you love and increase your sensitivity, so they can help anyone whose loved ones are distressed or under threat.

Leo – 23 July–23 August
Herb – saffron
Flower – marigold
Tree – laurel

These are natural substances of creativity and courage, and can provide these to anyone needing inspiration or a new perspective.

Virgo – 24 August–23 September
Herb – dandelion
Flower – pansy
Tree – almond

These are natural substances of practical application and high standards, and can offer support to anyone facing a testing time.

Libra – 24 September–23 October
Herb – mint
Flower – hydrangea
Tree – ash

These are natural substances of harmony and balance, and so are of use in trying to balance your inner and outer worlds.

Scorpio – 24 October–22 November
Herb – thyme
Flower – geranium
Tree – blackthorn

These are natural substances of passionate commitment and intense feelings, whether positive or negative, and so can be helpful in times of pressure or the need to perform well.

Sagittarius – 23 November–21 December
Herb – sage
Flower – carnation
Tree – oak

These are natural substances of curiosity and exploration, and can be helpful when you want to widen your horizons or bring more excitement into your life.

Capricorn – 22 December–20 January
Herb – comfrey
Flower – ivy
Tree – yew

These are natural substances of dogged determination and attention to detail, and are useful if you need to follow a slow and painstaking path.

Aquarius – 21 January–19 February
Herb – basil
Flower – orchid
Tree – flowering cherry

These are natural substances of independence and idealism, and so can be of help if you are striking out alone or have a dream to fulfil.

Pisces – 20 February–20 March
Herb – parsley
Flower – water lily
Tree – birch

These are natural substances of intuition and alternative perspectives, and so can help you to find an intuitive solution to conflicting demands.

If you live in warmer climes you can easily make substitutions with more exotic trees and flowers, and exchange spices for more traditional herbs. For example, a fig tree could be substituted for the willow, and an orange or lemon tree for the laurel. Look at the basic colours for each zodiacal sign and use these to guide you – golden flowers, herbs and trees for Leo, red ones for Aries and so on; for spices you can judge whether it is a hot or cool sign, leafy or more arid.

Floral and faunal magic

If it is tree magic you wish to use, you might want to make your spell in the place where the tree is growing, or use a small branch or twig of the tree as a magic wand to concentrate your energies. With flowers, you can either keep the relevant flowers in a vase at home or at work, or use a single bloom as part of a spell. Herbs can be either the fresh-growing or chopped plant, or the dried kind found in every kitchen. You can also buy flowers and herbs as oils, or burn them as incense. If a flower is out of season, choose another of similar colour or size.

Write to me, at my publisher, Foulsham, if you do discover any unusual herbs, flowers or trees that seem to work for you. I will add your information to a future book. Magic should be a living, growing tradition, and sometimes ancient practices no longer fit in the modern world. The ancients probably never intended their findings to be written in stone, and it was not until later periods when this information was collated that it was forced into a rigidity that was never intended.

An astrological herb and flower spell

- Justine is a Libran and her natural herb is mint, but she feels anything but harmonious, as she is having to choose between two options. She therefore decides to use the Piscean herb, parsley. Greg, her boyfriend, is a Piscean, so the herb has double significance. Justine bought some fresh parsley and mint from her local supermarket.

Should she accept the sudden proposal from Greg to marry him on special licence and fly to the Middle East? Her own work and personal options will be limited, but Greg has a very lucrative post on offer. Or should she stick with her college course in design that has a built-in promise of a job at the end?

Logic and common sense have flown out of the window, for Justine really loves Greg. It's a dilemma that can happen in any relationship where one partner has a job offer and the other needs to consider uprooting to be together.

Justine chopped the herbs roughly and mixed them together to blend the two aspects, adding water for intuition and the element of fire to heat the mixture and get her own inspirational powers going. (Witches of old made some foul brews.) All the while she visualised herself marrying Greg, flying to the Middle East and luxuriating in the hot sunshine. As the steam rose she added the element of air and logic, and then put the herbal soup in an earthenware pot for the earth and common sense.

Justine wanted to add flower magic and took a water lily (Greg's flower) from her pond. She picked the last of the hydrangeas, her zodiacal flower (though any large colourful bush flower would have done). She floated them both in a bowl of water, as a symbol of their love, realising as she did so that the hydrangea (her self) was out of its element and was becoming waterlogged. Justine realised, too, that she would be out of her element in a society where women occupy a different kind of role from that to which she is accustomed. As her concoction was edible (all herbs aren't – check in *Culpeper's Herbal*, published by Foulsham), she drank a spoonful. The herbs had cancelled out the flavour of each other; the resulting taste wasn't better but worse than the two separate ingredients.

She realised that if she married Greg at once they would both be worse off. The situation (the boiling) would bring out the worst in them both, as she would resent giving up her career at a crucial stage.

HYDRANGEA · WATER LILY

Was there a compromise? Justine bought some tiny plants of parsley and mint and planted them side by side, but not touching, in the garden. After a week, the time she needed to give Greg her decision, she noticed they had grown closer together; she realised that she and Greg still needed to grow separately before they could combine. And to her surprise, one last hydrangea she hadn't noticed had also bloomed. Justine told Greg she couldn't marry him and give up everything, but she would come out for holidays during the year he was away, and once she had completed her course she would think again about a permanent move.

Justine does have regrets, but has almost finished her course and is planning her first holiday. However, Greg has found the different way of life hard to take – after all, water lilies don't naturally thrive in deserts – and is cutting short his contract.

An astrological tree spell

• Judy needs to study chemistry as part of her joint degree. However, she can't seem to master the elemental tables she needs to learn, although she has no problems with other scientific subjects. Her birth sign is Capricorn, so she is not short of the dogged determination and application that are necessary for success in learning a subject.

What is the missing ingredient? – adaptability and, above all, a communication of her problem to people able to help, so hazel, the tree of Gemini, will perhaps soften the rigidity of her natural birth tree, the yew. Hazel trees are often used as magic wands. Judy cut a small twig of hazel from a tree in the garden of her halls of residence, and went off to the local park with a tree book to spot a row of stately yews.

She first walked clockwise round her yew tree holding her hazel wand in her left hand for right-brain inspiration. As she did so she visualised a circle of chemical symbols in bright yellow, a colour of communication, floating through a pale grey sky (air is the element of Gemini and pale grey its colour).

Next she picked a yew twig and bound it to her wand with strands of thick stalks and fronds growing near the yew. She stood on a bridge and cast it into the water. The parts did not split, but disappeared together in the centre of the fast-flowing stream. She then took a yew twig with fresh leaves and added one from her hazel tree, and decided to leave them on her window ledge throughout a whole moon cycle, for hidden inspiration and the creativity of the sun.

This spell was fast moving, however. On the way back from her spell she met her chemistry tutor, who had come over to see a student who wasn't at home. Judy explained her difficulties and her tutor suggested that she should attend some optional lectures that were run for members of the public, offering an intensive but very lively alternative introduction to the subject. Judy tried this, and soon saw the difficulties she was having stemmed from her own attempts to place the subject in the context of her previous scientific studies.

After a spell we will often meet just the right person to help, who 'just happens' to have a fruitless journey or cancelled appointment and seems particularly receptive. Magic doesn't operate in terms of cause and effect, but takes all kinds of byways. If a spell doesn't give the desired effect, perhaps it is a way of saying that the option we are eager for isn't the right one, and that a more open-ended spell may give us a third, unconsidered option.

Traditional flower magic

The rose is Venus's flower. Because the rose is magical and associated with love, it was a vital ingredient in traditional love spells. The spells still have charm, though their origins are lost in the mists of time.

To attract a desired lover, walk through a garden at midnight, scattering rose petals and softly calling the name of the lover.

Pick a rose on Midsummer Eve. Carry it home, walking backwards and not speaking a word. Fold it in white paper and keep it safe in a drawer until Christmas Day. Take it out of the paper and wear it to church. As you leave, your intended will come and take it from your bosom.

Gypsies have a belief that if a pregnant woman wants to know if she is carrying a boy or girl she should go to a garden where red and white roses are growing close together, and spin around the bushes sunwise 11 times, with eyes shut. She should then reach out, her eyes still closed, and pick a rose. If it is white the child will be a girl, if red a boy.

Marigolds, too, are associated with love and fidelity. Among the Southern Slavs, a girl will dig up the soil beneath her lover's footprints. On top she will plant a marigold. As the golden flowers bloom and grow, so shall her love.

HERB AND FLOWER DIVINATION

In the previous chapter, I introduced the idea of herb scrying, using kitchen herbs. However, growing herbs and flowers has traditionally also been a powerful form of divination, practised by women from early times.

Where love is concerned, logic sometimes flies out of the window. Deep down we may know the answer. Love divination can help us to reach this knowledge. Take two carrots and cut the tops off. Place each on a saucer and label one 'Yes', one 'No', or as appropriate for you. The first to sprout gives you your answer.

A faster variant to use is mustard and cress. Plant in two (or more) flattish pots and again label with the options. The first to sprout or show the most growth is the correct option. If neither grows the choice may be neither, or to wait.

Traditionally, maidens would leave onions by the fire to sprout, but this is a bit pungent for modern tastes.

While your plants are making the decision, do not think about the issue or discuss it with others. Try to make the growing days fruitful, by taking up a new activity or maybe spending a bit of time alone to give yourself confidence.

The oldest kind of flower divination is using the dandelion, known as the oracle, the flower of prophecy. Blowing a dandelion clock and saying alternately 'Yes'/'No' or 'Go'/'Stay', whatever the dilemma, is still very popular. Rose petals are often plucked for love matters, while the daisy, whose meaning is innocence, can also be used, and then bound into a chain as a symbol of enduring love or friendship.

TRADITIONAL TREE MAGIC

Trees have been regarded as sacred in all cultures, and even today, as we hang our evergreen boughs at Christmas or decorate maypoles with ribbons and wreaths on May Day, we recall those ancient beliefs.

The oak, the king of trees, has been revered from ancient times. Sacred to Thor, the god of thunder, because it is a tree often struck by lightning, it is seen in many traditions as the most magical of trees. The classical world also recognised its supremacy. At Dodona, the earliest of the Grecian sacred groves, Zeus was worshipped in his sacred tree. This oracular tree in the grove of oaks was consulted through the rustling of its leaves, the murmur of the spring at its roots, and by the oak logs kept at its base. The dead wood was said to retain these oracular properties; Jason's ship contained a beam which gave the Argonauts advice.

The sacred oak of Jupiter was worshipped on the Capitoline Hill in Rome, and again was a source of wisdom from the gods. To the Druids the oak was their special tree. Indeed, Druid means 'knowledge of the oak' (*wid* – knowledge, *dru* – oak). He who has knowledge of the oak is said to be able to attract the power of the elements for his own use, and to control storms.

The space between two oaks was said to be the doorway to unseen realms, where faeries and other wondrous creatures live.

Traditional tree spells

To remove bad feelings:
Find a hazel, oak, elm and willow twig and hold each in the smoke of a fire, repeating seven times,

'Turner be turned,
Burner be burned,
Let only good,
Come of this wood.'

Spit on each twig, break it in three and throw each into the fire. As the fire dies down, so the bad feelings will lose their power.

For good luck:
Pick an evenly divided ash leaf and say,

'Even ash I do thee pluck,
Hoping thus to meet good luck.'

This talisman was traditionally worn in a hat or as a buttonhole.

Tree healing

For children with rickets, hernias or wounds that would not heal, an ash tree was split and the child passed through it nine times. The tree was bound up, and when the tree healed, so would the child.

You can use this technique to heal quarrels and emotional ills. Find an ash tree with a split branch, and pass a copper coin through it for love, seeing the breach or unhappiness being mended. Now tie up the tree with a piece of string and go and put the quarrel right.

Modern tree spells: a spell for strengthening your own identity

You may feel temporarily lacking in confidence and doubting your own worth. This may be due to a broken relationship, a setback at work or the erosion of your identity by the needs of others. This spell is best performed at mid-morning on a clear day, near an oak or other large tree which is a symbol of identity and independence.

Hold a mirror in your left hand (for intuitive right-brain intervention) so that you can see the tree over your shoulder, and chant softly or say within yourself 'I exist, separate from others and from this symbol'. Walk round the inside of a circle, and be aware that you are part of the past and the present.

Place your hands in contact with the tree and ask for a glimpse of the future you will share. You will see, either as a dream, a vision or in your mind's eye, not a set future, but one of the paths you have the option to tread, and the strong person you are inside.

Take an acorn or a twig of the tree to plant in your garden if you have one, or in an open space that needs adornment. Each morning look in the mirror and see your unique beauty and worth. Remember the oak tree when your identity is under threat, or your beliefs and integrity come into question.

As your own mighty oak grows from that small acorn, or maybe founders and needs replacing, remember that you are of worth, and however slow progress may be, you are a unique part of nature and the universe.

As you touch wood for luck, remember the dryads and hamadryads, tree nymphs who reside within trees and are said to die when a tree is cut down.

A tree ritual with a friend

If you are working with friend or partner, take two cords, one for each of your wishes. If you share the same desire, you can use a double cord. For this, a traditional nine-foot length may be best. An oak tree or any other sturdy tree will do. As you come together sunwise to tie or loop the knots, embrace the tree, and if you wish, recite in turn your desires. Move to and from the tree rhythmically, seeing the power rising from the roots, and chorusing nine times,

> 'Empowering tree,
> Rise into me,
> Knot binding,
> Knot finding,
> Knot winding,
> Power free.'

Let go of the cords if looped, and untie the knots moon-wise, chanting 'Fly free' in a crescendo. Hang your wish cord above your bed until the next new moon.

If you have a group of friends who are working towards a collective need, such as healing an absent person or preserving a threatened area of land or wildlife habitat, you may wish to make a wheel of cords around the tree, looping them rather than tying. Whirl round faster and faster, sunwise, chanting,

> 'Oak heal, oak wheel,
> Knot I tie, power fly.'

Call this nine times, then pause, count nine and chant again. Repeat this until you feel that you have reached a climax of energy, and let the cords free.

You may find you spontaneously continue to dance. There are natural spirals around an old tree, and our footsteps are guided if we trust our intuitions. The most powerful circle dancing frequently involves a simple stem-and-stamp rhythm, that harmonises with rhythms etched into the earth over the centuries.

Remember you are not raising any dark or external energies in your knot rituals, only those natural forces intrinsic in the earth, of which we are part, and our own inner powers of light and life. However, you may prefer to do this in a garden or in a wood in early morning, where you will be undisturbed.

TRADITIONAL TREE-RELATED DIVINATION

Pick 30 sticks of about the same length, about 6–8 in. from an oak grove, and mark one side with a cross, or scrape away the bark. Place a light-coloured tablecloth beneath an oak tree and think of a 'Yes'/'No', 'Go'/'Stay' or 'Act'/'Wait' option. Cast your sticks at the same time, and count the number that show the marked or bark-free side, which I interpret as the positive side, but you may view in the opposite way.

In this system if there are more 'Yeses' than 'Nos', you know that deep down that is what your inner voice is telling you. Note how close the numbers are, whether they are fairly evenly matched. If you have exactly the same number positive and negative, then the issue is not clear cut. Try rephrasing the question.

At Hallowe'en, float a piece of wood from a beech tree in a bowl by your bedside. You will dream of falling off a bridge into a river, and your true love will come and rescue you.

Sew eight holly leaves to your nightie at the midwinter solstice and you will dream of your true love.

Finally the best magic is to hold any tree and feel its magical energy flowing into you. Circle it sunwise, all the time chanting your wish and touching the four points, north, south, east and west, as you pass by. Then take a leaf and on it scratch your wish with a twig from the tree. Cast the leaf into running water and go out and make it come true.

MAGIC IN THE WORKPLACE

The principles of magic are the same in the working environment as they are in the garden or home. However, because in a conventional workplace we may be working with colleagues with whom we may not always feel in tune, and because opportunities for solitude are fewer, workplace magic needs to be more protective and more subtle.

SYMPATHETIC WORKPLACE MAGIC

Sympathetic magic involves using a symbol to represent what you want, on the principle of like attracting like – a toy train or plane for long-distance travel, for example. In workplace spells you may find a charm bracelet valuable; a silver charm in the shape of a key could be used if you are seeking to open new doors for promotion. Alternatively, pictures in a magazine or brochure can be circled as a focus for spells.

The elements, too, can be adapted to incorporate objects that are routinely found in offices, factories and shops:

Earth – a packet of paper clips can represent the metals that are mined from the earth. You can even make your circle from them. Or use a metal pen, a wooden ruler or some flowers, even paper or wood chippings.

Air – you can use a pot-pourri air freshener or a small electric fan.

Fire – can be a lamp, a pocket torch or a make-up mirror.

Water – can be represented by a small vase of flowers, or even a paper cup of coffee or juice.

For an impromptu wand buy two small quartz crystals, one clear and pointed, the other a rounded milky quartz or snow quartz. You can use these crystals to hold papers down, and can hold the clear crystal in your right hand to give you energy and inspiration, or the cloudy one in your left if you feel agitated, to bring calm. Alternatively, wear a quartz pendant, pointed at one end, that can double for dowsing.

When you've got a problem or issue to be resolved at work, draw a circle on paper or visualise one, remembering to move clockwise or sunwise as you create it.

Place your earth symbol in the north, your air sign in the east, your fire in the south and your water in the west. In the centre use a small symbol or picture as a focus for your need.

However, if you wish, you can carry out the whole process symbolically, by marking letters to represent the four main compass points, and writing in the centre of the circle a word or phrase to represent your desire.

Pass the symbol round the circle, or say in your mind the symbolic word, through the four elements in turn, clockwise for a wish, anti-clockwise to get rid of something unwanted in your working life.

Begin with the north, mentally calling on the icy power of this region as you visualise ice floes and icebergs to cut through inaction. Then, if you're going clockwise, invoke the winds of the eastern plains to blow you where you want to be, clearing your mind and filling you with direction. The warm southern sun will melt any opposition and give you the power to communicate. Finally, the cool green waters of the west will summon your intuitive powers and ability to reach below the surface to the heart of the matter.

Finally, as you hold your symbol or symbolic words, see yourself in the centre of things, perfectly balanced with the cool breeze and the gentle sun warming the water, and live'in your mind the pleasures of what it is you have achieved. See yourself as you are now, not in some illusory, perfect state – that's where much magic falls down. You can be happy as you are now, with the same looks, the same friends, the same imperfections and strengths. Be glad you are what you are.

After your magic go for a walk in the fresh air if you can, to a local park or open space – ten to one you'll see your symbol in actuality before you've been out two minutes.

OVERCOMING
WORKPLACE HAZARDS

Often the actual tasks of the day are challenging, and problems only come with the people we encounter, difficult clients or customers, a bitchy or autocratic boss, sniping colleagues, or lazy or incompetent juniors whose burden we end up shouldering. Our own self-image can be dented by such encounters, and we can end up quite irrationally feeling guilty and inadequate.

Protecting our self-image at work

Create an invisible magic circle of golden thread round your-self, a space where you are safe and untouchable. Collect together all your negative feelings about an encounter or ongoing relationship with your boss, colleagues, employees or customers. Make your negative emotions into a long silver cord and fashion it into a star. Throw your star as far as you can into the sky – you can do this mentally or stretch your arms. If you look out of the window, you will see a shimmering on the greyest day, as your negative vibes are transformed into the beautiful stardust we need for wishes.

Now for the inner fears that fuel any conflict, that you aren't as competent, as clever, as witty as ... – the list of your own shortcomings stretches back long before work, to the pushchair. Maybe Mum and Dad told you right from the beginning that you weren't as dainty as your little sister or as clever as your cousin down the road. Teachers, no doubt, added to the list. Some of us, myself included, however competent and successful on the surface, hear that echo from the past, and interpret suggestions as criticisms, questioning of our ideas as a rejection of ourselves.

Transform your self doubts into a series of shimmering sunbeams, and direct them one by one back to the sun to con-vert into positive rays of your future unfolding potential. You can use a make-up mirror for your star or sunbeams to project rays, if your inner vision is daunted by the task, or it is an over-cast day. Your new psychic confidence will easily translate into your working environment, making you appear more assured, more vibrant, more assertive, whatever your area of perceived inadequacy, and will invite positive responses from others.

It's not just ordinary people who have this inner well of doubt. Many actors feel they shine only on stage. Top athletes see their success purely in terms of what they can do on the track, and supermodels, in spite of the accolades, worry about every blemish, fearing that they are overweight and un-attractive.

You may need to place your circle around yourself for quite a while and repeat the sunbeam technique. However, gradually your inner radiance will replace the uncertainty within, and your corresponding outer vibrancy will meet with approval from others, even from those who previously seemed to ignore or dislike you.

A psychic 'electric fence'

However, no matter how confident and positive you are, there will always be those people who will still find fault and be snide, because their own inner world leaves them unable to relate to others except in terms of a power struggle. To protect yourself against such souls, who seem to sap your very essence, you will need a psychic 'electric fence' round your outer limits.

Much is written about etheric bodies and auras – there's believed to be a spiritual energy field beyond and in the shape of your body that makes you go 'ouch' if someone collides mentally or psychically with you, or barges into your space.

Whether you perceive this idea as actuality or as a metaphor for our unique inner essence, you can put up an electric fence if you feel your golden circle fading before sapping negativity at work. The electric fence is more elliptic, more jagged than the circle we used to boost our self-image. It ensures that your essence remains untouched even from the most vitriolic attack.

You can hear your fence crackle and see it like a golden zig-zag in yellows and orange. Draw it in your mind's eye – leave plenty of space, a good six inches at least all round. Make sure it is continuous, no breaks or gaps for the odd niggle or put-down to wriggle through. This jagged body shape may not look like a circle, but the magic circle principle is the same.

If you wish to escape alone to the cloakroom, you can use the clear creative end of your quartz crystal to trace your golden boundary. Stand in front of a mirror and concentrate on your inner and outer beauty, strength, intelligence and power. Look at yourself with love and acceptance, and you will be strong. If you can't escape from your pursuer, draw the shape mentally or as a doodle on a notepad.

Your electric fence is not too highly charged – you can't go round psychically electrocuting everyone who makes a crass

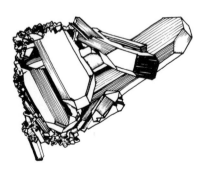

or unkind remark. But the nasty tingling colleagues, superiors or clients feel but can't explain when they tell you something 'for your own good', will keep them at a distance, and they will be less eager to offload their spite or anger on you.

CREATING YOUR
PERSONAL WORK SPACE

However, even friendly encounters can on occasions intrude, when you need time and space to concentrate on a project. A particular person may insist on chattering nineteen to the dozen about their social life. A senior colleague may constantly watch over your shoulder, offering so many helpful suggestions that they become counter-productive, because they spoil your concentration and divert you from developing your own style.

You don't want to hurt or offend, but simply to create at certain times a space round you where you can work undisturbed. This can be especially helpful in a noisy environment.

When you need space, use a protective crystal, such as jet, amber, tiger's eye, lapis lazuli, jasper, coral, or a small piece of clear crystal quartz, kept for such occasions in your drawer, on your workbench or in your locker, or wear one as a pendant. You can use your crystal wand as a paperweight, keeping the receptive end facing the door or entry point of any likely source of interruption or trouble.

Finally, you need a psychic shield to ensure that you remain calm in your own work, no matter what crises or challenges arise to set your colleagues panicking during the day. Some people make a career out of magnifying crises or problems, or insisting on sharing the latest piece of 'who said what'.

The psychic shield is an ancient earth symbol, and if you make a shiny shield you can use it as a mirror to reflect back any intrusions, so the interruption is deflected or diverted to someone less busy.

The psychic shield technique originated when Alexander the Great went into the Valley of Diamonds, which was guarded by snakes with the power to kill with a glance (you may have some in your workplace). The serpents were overcome by the polished shields of his soldiers, and Alexander got away with the loot.

You can use any shiny substance – the lid of a small container, a make-up mirror, even your spare glasses – placed between you and the entry point of any potential disturbance, or wear silvery earrings or a pendant. Silver is the colour of the moon and so is a focus for your unconscious powers.

Should you sense potential strife that will involve you refereeing or getting involved in office politics at an inopportune moment, hold your glasses or pendant and visualise the sun glinting on your psychic shield and mirroring back any negativity. Smile a welcome to whoever is moving towards your space, letting the gentle light beams carry them towards a more receptive target. See their words emanating as sunbeams and respond accordingly, so they feel satisfied by the brief encounter.

CREATING A PSYCHICALLY FRIENDLY WORKPLACE

It is also possible, once you are confident of your own psychic strength and protective devices, to make your workplace more happy and harmonious, and this is just as important if you are one of the millions of people who now work from a home office. For starters, try a rainbow.

Making a rainbow

Rainbow crystals are highly prized by the Aborigines, and in former times rainbows were seen by Norse warriors as a bridge across the dimensions. The crock of gold got added later, but you might like to imagine yours spilling gold and silver dust to lighten any grey sludge clouds around you. If you're very lucky there might be a shower of rain followed by a burst of sunshine outside. If so, silently invite it in and, if possible, open the window.

However, even on the darkest winter day, you can use your inner rainbow. It's said that we all have within us energy centres, sometimes called *chakras*, that whirl round and contain certain colours. I love the idea of all those internal firework displays going on as we stand jammed in the subway trying to avoid one another's eyes.

Whether or not you go along with this theory, it makes sense that we have inner energies that can be galvanised to affect our outer world. You can create many different rainbows, made of flowers, lotus petals, even birds, starting from dark earth energies near your spine and synthesising as pure white light pouring out of the top of your head. I'll start with an adaptation of the chakra concept and your own creativity can improve on it. One woman I know sees her protective rainbow made up of multi-coloured ducks, and people comment on her lovely smile.

Red is the colour of what is called sometimes the root chakra, which is located at the base of your spine, and you can think of it as your instinctive survival colour. Set this whirling and see a red semi-circle circle around the work area, giving an energetic, enthusiastic atmosphere.

Now add *orange*, that lurks around your pelvis area, those energies sometimes connected with sexuality but which in the work context emphasise the right of everyone to be what they are. Let this semi-circle of identity give everyone the ability not to want to interfere or upset the lives and psyches of others.

Next round the solar plexus, just above the navel, is a clear *yellow*, communicating energy. This communicates only positive matters, praise, support and encouragement. It balances issues, assimilating what is positive and vital, and eliminating the irrelevant or destructive. Get these three whizzing round and already you feel happier and the energies lighter.

Green is located mid-point on a level with your heart, whose beat instantly becomes more regular as you relax. This colour brings lots of friendship, tones down rivalry and makes for acceptance of others' foibles and irritating ways.

Blue comes from your throat area and rises up your face, relieving your tense neck muscles and tightness of the throat. Blue is about speaking truth, but for now is tempered with kindness and altruism. It abolishes gossip and back-biting, and suggests improvements in the working conditions for everyone.

Add a *deep violet* from between your eyes at brow level, and finish off with the lot spiralling from the top of your head into the *white* that they become. This calls into play your unconscious wisdom, your intuition and all that lovely clear energy that will have you bounding home for whatever constitutes a good time.

Use this magic rainbow first thing in the morning, after lunch and when you go home, so the place won't seethe overnight with discarded irritations. You might like to make an actual crystal rainbow, perhaps a red carnelian or jasper, an amber, a yellow citrine, a piece of green jade or aventurine, a dyed blue howzite or turquoise, an amethyst or piece of sugilite, and finally a clear crystal quartz. You can use small pieces kept in a bag and spread them out in a semi-circle when you feel the atmosphere getting gloomy or fraught.

WORKPLACE SPELLS

A computer spell

If you are adept with a drawing programme on your computer, set up the circle and the element points on the screen, draw the focus in the centre of the circle, and manipulate it through the compass points with your mouse. Remember to make your circle clockwise; the principles apply even if you are drawing your circle on a computer screen.

- Jenny was anxious to get a new contract that would involve her designing a campaign to help the hospital where she worked promote a new women's screening programme. However, interests were entrenched, and she knew that the man favoured by the management committee had very little knowledge of the illnesses involved, saw the campaign purely in terms of finance, and believed it could be run very cheaply as part of a wider programme of improvements.

Jenny drew a circle clockwise on her screen, seeing her own ideas flowing from the screen on to hoardings and leaflets. In the north of the circle she drew an unfolding flower, for she knew her ideas had solid foundation and would expand over the months in a practical way. In the east she created an arrow with her mouse, certain her ideas were targeted and would reach the right audience. In the south she drew a sun, with rays streaking out in all directions, inspiring women to come forward to take advantage of the facilities offered, confident that early diagnosis would save lives.

Finally, in the west, Jenny pictured a stream that grew into a wide river and eventually fell as a waterfall, showing that the scheme could begin in a modest way with the available resources, and that as it succeeded it would naturally attract resources.

Her mouse slipped and the images merged in the centre. Suddenly Jenny saw the logo for the campaign within a circle, and the four salient points. She created there and then a new inspired proposal, and to her amazement managed to talk the committee into offering her six months' secondment, to manage as well as to design the scheme.

Magical mechanics

When a computer or piece of machinery breaks down, it is usually at a crucial point, just after any service personnel have left for home.

If the need is urgent, remember the concept of expanding possibility. Take a dark crystal such as a smoky quartz to remove any blockages in the system. Trace a square shape clockwise in the air, starting in the left corner of the top side, enclosing the object that won't work. A square is a symbol of the four elements and the spiritual world enclosed in time and matter. Since it's a practical issue, a square is more effective than a circle.

Keep tracing an invisible line around the actual outline of the broken computer, grass-cutter or whatever is your current unco-operative object. Draw a doorway midway in the south side of the square to let out the negative force contained in the dark crystal. Pull it like a long, dark, grey cord, wind it into a ball and toss it into the sky to make a star.

You no longer need the square, so reverse the invisible square anti-clockwise, again starting at the top left. You should end up where you began. Using a clear crystal – the *yang* or positive energy to the *yin* of the dark crystal – inject some white, pure energy into the stubborn object. This time see the shape as you fill it expanding with bubbling white foam or light. It's always important to replace anything you take away with something positive, and this is true of life as well as magic, to stop the old negativity, whether doubt, regrets or an inert hard disk, coming creeping back.

As you do this, see the screen come to life or the motor starting. At the precise moment it reaches full power, switch on in the outside world.

Get the machine serviced as soon as possible; psychic repairs are usually only temporary.

DIVINATION AT WORK

There are many decisions that have to be made during a working day and about work-related issues. Intuitive decisions are part of a woman's working armoury. Indeed, most very successful business people, male or female, have an instinct for making the right decision, almost a sixth sense. A female solicitor I met at a businesswomen's lunch told me she relied very strongly on her intuition in summing up new clients, and invariably the facts supported her judgement. Indeed, two Harvard University studies showed groups of students videos of professors, and asked them to rate their effectiveness as teachers. Some students saw the tapes for ten seconds, others for only two seconds. These first impression ratings were virtually identical to judgements made by students who had been taught by the academic staff for a term.

However, it can be very difficult to rely on intuition if it goes against the opinion of others, or evidence collected by more conventional means. In any workplace, however, there are objects and tools that can be used to confirm the rightness of an instinctive decision. In Chapter 10, I suggest some methods of dowsing for decisions that are equally effective in the business or personal sphere.

Yes/No divination

The simplest way is to keep a plastic tube of 20 small erasers, the kind with just the brand name stamped on the front. If the erasers are blank, draw a symbol on one side to mark a positive response. Concentrate on the option question, 'Yes'/'No', 'Act'/'Wait', 'Sign'/'Do not sign', and closing your eyes tip the erasers on to a table, workbench or desk.

Count the number of marked sides uppermost. If the number of marked and unmarked sides is even, then rephrase the question.

More complex options

You can ask a whole series of questions in this way, each time using the first question that comes into your head and throwing your erasers to get a positive or negative response. You can resolve quite complex work issues like this.

If you get an even number, it is an indication that the question you are asking may not be the real issue, so you should try a different one. Some people use a proper flowchart system, the left hand column for 'Yes', the middle one for 'Ask again' and the right for 'No'. You simply write the questions after the initial one in the appropriate column. However, you can also just write your questions as a long list, with the numbers in brackets, giving the 'Yes' number first, or 'Y', 'N', or 'R' (re-phrase). If a choice is very close you may need to ask more questions until the issue becomes clear-cut.

• Pauline has just qualified as a chartered accountant to the delight of her parents, and has been offered a position in the firm of one of their friends, with a good salary and chances of a partnership after a few years.

But Pauline has become involved in an enterprise organising children's parties, from the catering to the entertainment, with Amy, a friend who has recently qualified at catering college. Recently they have been turning down a lot of work, and Amy has suggested that they start a business together.

Pauline hates accountancy, but has just saved the deposit for a flat, and her parents cannot believe she would throw away the opportunity of a lifetime. She takes 20 blank erasers and draws a butterfly on one side of each, which she sees as freedom. The first number listed represents the yes choice. Keep asking until you have resolved the question in your own mind.

Question 1. Should I take up Amy's option? 10/10 R.
Question 2. Do I want to take up Amy's option? 12/8 Y.
Question 3. Am I worried about security? 5/15 N.
(This answer was a surprise to Pauline.)
Question 4. Am I worried about my parents' disapproval? 18/2 Y.
Question 5. Should I be worried about my parents' approval? 4/16 N.
Question 6. Should I combine the two careers? 20/0 Y.
(This was obviously the answer, but how?)
Question 7. Should I change the emphasis? 18/2 Y.
Question 8. Should I work part-time at accountancy? 17/3 Y.
Question 9. Should I do accountancy freelance? 18/2 Y.

But was this possible? Pauline went along to a business agency and found that, unlike other fields, there were plenty of opportunities for a freelance accountant, especially to audit the accounts of small self-employed businesses. She decided to move in with Amy for a few months and give the business a try, and with an enterprise grant, set up. Pauline realised that linked with the business issue was the need to move her working and personal life away from the direct influence of her well-meaning but possessive parents.

Working in her parents' friend's firm was not a viable option, even if the party option had not existed. She knows that her parents are not happy with her decision, but is confident that she can succeed. Living out other people's dreams or ideal worlds rarely works, but it is easy to be stifled and this can lead to regrets.

Telephone divination

If you need more focused direction about an issue and the way to respond, try using telephone numbers as a modern form of numerology or number magic. Numerology, or significant numbers, dates back to the Ancient Egyptians, and was practised in many cultures, including the Judaic. Numbering the letters in one's own name can be very limiting for a spontaneous situation.

However, if you pick a telephone number that appears at a significant moment in your work life, it can trigger your unconscious radar to alert you to the best action. For example, there might be a number left on your answering machine or one on the top of a letter you have just opened.

If there isn't an obvious spontaneous number, close your eyes, open a telephone directory at random, and run your finger down the page until you feel one is right. The process involves a mixture of telekinesis (the ability to affect objects by thought), telepathy (mind communication) and 'synchronicity' (what Jung would call a 'meaningful coincidence', when an outer symbol reflects your inner state). Write down the number and add up the numbers from left to right, until you are left with two. Add these to give a single digit. Even within numerology there are many variations of the meanings of numbers 1-9, so I have combined the best of what seem to be conflicting systems in a way that relates to career and work issues rather than relationships. However, you can adapt them to the personal sphere. If you feel a number has a particular significance for you, or is fortunate, then go along with your own unique world view.

1 – is the number of new beginnings, new projects or an innovative approach. Go for the original solution and try to get new input.

2 – involves balancing two options or demands, and says it's important to sort out your immediate priorities. If two colleagues or employees have widely differing opinions, try to find a compromise.

3 – says you should expand your horizons and options and seek something more than is on offer. Be prepared to make a considerable input and put in hard work that may only bear fruit later.

4 – involves seeking a practical solution and accepting that at present there are limitations in your plans. Make sure any schemes have a firm foundation, and that the background is adequately researched.

5 – is the number of perhaps striking out alone, seeking an alternative solution, communicating clearly, and above all, seeing the situation in terms of gains rather than losses.

6 – speaks of harmony, and says it's important to make yourself as well as others happy. Consolidate achievements and make sure your efforts are noticed.

7 – deals with your unconscious mind, and says you should be aware of what is going on under the surface in your dealings with others. Use intuition, especially in summing up new clients or workmates, as they may not be quite what they seem.

8 – says that caution is the keynote and the conventional path may be right at the moment. Don't take any short cuts, and follow all the necessary legal and safety regulations.

9 – is the number of courage and determination, and says that if you stick at things you will succeed. It may seem that you will never reach your target, so it may be time to shed a few unnecessary burdens and make sure everyone does his/her share.

If it is an important decision or you are uncertain that the suggestion seems right, pick a second number and see what insights that adds. You can even try a third.

Mobile phone divination

- Megan was due for promotion, which would involve many more hours travelling and several days a month 'on the road'. Her boyfriend was very unenthusiastic about the new job, and said she would find it too much of a strain as they were hoping to marry and have a family in a couple of years. He said she would only be able to work part-time once they had children, so her efforts would be wasted.

On the morning of the interview, Megan found a 'call waiting' number on her mobile phone and added up the number. It came to 2, suggesting that it was a choice between her relationship and having the career she wanted.

Uncertain, she used the phone number of the firm she was hoping to join. This time it came up with 9 altogether, telling her that she needed courage and determination if she was to fulfil her potential.

Still worried, she picked a phone number on the side of the bus, advertising a travel firm, and came up with another 2, which confirmed what Megan knew in her heart. Whatever the outcome of the interview, the conventional future her boyfriend was moving towards wasn't one she was ready for. Megan was offered the job, and while she was away on her initial training course her boyfriend met someone new, whom he married shortly after. Megan is alone but happy.

Coloured pencil or felt-tip divination

Take 11 felt tips or coloured pencils and place them in a pencil case or box. When you have a decision to make or need to work out a strategy, shake the closed case or box and pull out three colours without looking.

The first, the key issue, tells you the real area of concern, which may not be the surface one. The second, the strategy colour, suggests the best approach. The third, the probable outcome, offers a possible result of carrying through your decision or strategy.

If you are dealing with a person, the colours will give you an insight into their real feelings.

White – is the change colour, suggesting that radical approaches and novel remedies will be best.

Black – is the colour of negativity and says there is a lot of opposition or concern to be allayed.

Grey – is the colour of compromise and implies that negotiation is the answer.

Red – warns against confrontation, as there may be a lot of strong feelings flying.

Orange – suggests that this is a matter where identity and status are at stake, so be sure to build up the ego of anyone involved.

Yellow – implies that communication may not be clear; it's important to spell out the facts and your position to avoid any misunderstanding.

Green – says it's a time to beware emotional demands or appeals to sentiment that may not be appropriate in business affairs.

Blue – suggests that it's important to pay attention to detail and the small print and use a conventional approach.

Purple – talks of using intuition and following gut feelings.

Silver – says beware the easy path and watch out for back-stabbing.

Gold – is for altruism, a time not to worry about getting the credit or scoring points, but looking at the long-term goal.

You can also use this method with coloured rubber bands or pieces of ribbon.

Laura's crayon divination

- Laura is an artist in her early thirties working in a large design office. She has applied for promotion but knows that her immediate boss, Susan, who is almost at retirement age, feels she is being disloyal wishing to change departments after she has helped her so much.

Laura picks a green, an orange and a yellow crayon. She realises that her boss, who is not married and lives for the office, feels emotionally rebuffed by her because she wishes to move on, and that she must reassure Susan that they will still work together and that it is her boss's efforts that will be repaid in Laura's promotion. The fact that the green is the key suggests that the problem is an emotional one, and will have to be handled carefully.

Orange represents the best strategy, so Laura needs to make her boss feel she is not being threatened by her potential promotion, but that it reflects on her own excellent training abilities. Laura needs to allay her boss's fears of being redundant in her career, and can ask Susan's advice about the interview so she feels involved. The yellow for the possible outcome implies that if Laura does get the job, which will rank equally with Susan's, they will be able to communicate more easily, and as repayment for Susan's help in the past, perhaps Laura can help to steer her towards facing her own future, her impending retirement.

MAGIC WHILE
TRAVELLING

❧

In times gone by travelling was a hazardous process, and so a whole variety of superstitions and protective rituals grew up. For example, the origin of the St Christopher medallion, to protect travellers, lies in the belief that before he was martyred, Christopher asked God to protect anywhere his body lay from plague, pestilence and other misfortunes. For this reason, pictures of St Christopher would be hung in public places, and icons and St Christopher carvings erected near gateways and entrances to towns and churches. Gradually, St Christopher's image, transposed on to a medallion, came to be carried by travellers as protection.

Modern travel dangers are very different, but nevertheless we can still feel vulnerable, especially late at night.

PROTECTION WHILE TRAVELLING

Even with the best precautions, you can find yourself alone in a dark or potentially threatening place, or feel anxious and under threat when travelling after dark or alone, especially in big cities. There are many publicised precautions that can be taken to minimise risk. Psychic protection can be a useful addition to earthly action, both in minimising your vulnerability and visibility to anyone who would do you harm, and making you feel more confident of your safety when you are alone outside your home or workplace.

Garnet is traditionally associated with safety when travelling, as is the bloodstone, and they are believed to lower your outer signals to any hostile forces. You will not literally become invisible, but you may find that you are less noticeable and blend into the background.

Sceptics would say that if you have your protective talisman you feel less anxious and so don't give off 'victim vibes'. Whatever the 'facts', these crystals seem to have offered some protection to travellers over the centuries. St Christopher medallions, or turquoise fastened to clothing, are other ancient amulets that translate well for safe passage through today's urban hazards.

Creative companions

If you find yourself leaving work late and have to go through a dimly-lit, deserted foyer, or are alone in a railway carriage and can't move nearer the guard until the next station, fill the threatening space or carriage with images of friends or family. When you get home you may find they say they were thinking of you strongly at the time you linked in with them.

People a deserted early-morning street or late-night taxi rank with a market, whether creatures of your psyche or imprints of another age. Look at the stalls and savour the scents and sounds of an earlier era. Call up a knight in armour and get him to walk down the subway steps with you, swinging his battle-axe. Invite an Amazonian warrior or Boudicca in full woad, to share your journey.

Creating a safe path

Place a soft grey mist around your outline and walk with con-fidence towards your destination, seeing it quite clearly in your mind's eye even if it is physically out of view. Erect steep cliff-walls round your path. Your footprints may seem unusually silent – it's part of the protective magical aura you are creating. Keep to the clear, bright, narrow passage you have made towards the opening of light; the rock will close behind you to deter unfriendly followers.

One woman I know used to put her little daughter into a hypnotic trance when they were walking home through the black-out during the Second World War, by creating the scenes of films she'd seen. This moving picture show worked, and the distance of several miles would pass in moments. The only problem, her daughter Lilian told me, was that it ruined seeing the films when she grew up, as her mother hadn't missed out a single detail.

THE PSYCHIC
BREAKDOWN SERVICE

What if your car suddenly stops in the middle of nowhere, or you notice the petrol gauge is reading empty and it's miles to the nearest garage? If it's dark and raining and there are no houses for miles, a bit of psychic assistance may keep you safe till help arrives, or better still, get you home or to a friendly mechanic.

Of course, in an ideal world we check petrol levels and so on regularly, and carry a mobile phone that never gets out of range. Even then cars go wrong, however, and the spare part you need is the one you don't carry, or a garage unexpectedly closes early – where I live, the only one on the Isle of Wight serving petrol after 10 p.m. ceased trading the evening I was returning home from a late-night radio show on the mainland.

Explain your need to the cosmos and maybe make a mental offer – for example, you'll phone a difficult relative for a chat, or sort out some unwanted bric-à-brac with a smile when the local Brownies come knocking.

If your car breaks down, visualise solid gold petrol pumps just over the hill, or a guy or gal from the breakdown patrol who just remembers he's got to pop in and see his or her old auntie about half a mile from where you are puzzling over the unresponsive engine with your fast-fading torch.

Raise a bit of red energy from the base of your spine, your basic survival power, and fashion it into a giant, glowing, ruby starting handle, the kind you see on vintage cars in cartoons. Whirl it round in your mind so fast it changes through deep red to pale pink and back again, and gives off brilliant red sparks. As you do this get into your car and start it up the moment the psychic power is at its greatest, like a plane on the runway, busting a gut to take off.

Don't forget to take off the brake or pause to be surprised, or you'll lose the momentum. Keep the psychic power flowing in a thin coil. Keep explaining to the car that this really is an emergency, and that the engine has to run at least until you find a bit of mortal aid. Don't forget to say please, and radiate love and positivity over your beloved vehicle.

Offer encouragement to the absent garage attendant who will have broken the habits of a lifetime and kept the station open later than usual, and to the mechanic who won't be on tea break, off sick or have left early for the bank holiday. He or she will have just the part you need incredibly cheaply, and will fix it there and then, with a smile. Don't let doubt creep in.

Praise your car for its reliability and endurance – even offer to clean it on your next free Sunday – and thank your rescuer in advance.

Give your car wings, paddles if there's a nearby river. Raise it slightly so its wheels hardly touch the road. Make the road golden like a moving walkway so the miles just slip by without effort. Don't waste vital energies on 'what ifs' and free-floating panic. If you know the road, use an internal psychic magnet to draw the familiar landmarks nearer, or concentrate on walking through your front door and telling everyone how you nearly didn't make it.

- Dorothy, who is now in her 80s, told me how she visited an exhibition at Olympia in London from her home in Bracknell with three young friends. When they finally returned to the car late it in the evening, it would not start; the battery was totally unresponsive. After about 20 minutes the two young men were about to give up and phone a garage. This would have cost a fortune, since the driver was not a member of a breakdown service.

Dorothy suggested to Sue that they sat on the wall and concentrated hard on the car starting. The men mocked, but after a short time Dorothy told the driver to try the car again. Laughing, he did so; the car started first time and behaved beautifully all the way home.

Few people, outside the Uri Geller league, can do these things to order, but many women can recall at least one occasion when the car magically started, or a missing set of car keys turned up at the crucial moment.

PSYCHIC MAP READING

Another hazard of travelling is getting lost. You can make a pendulum using a key on a piece of string, for working out the right direction. If you end up driving through a maze of deserted streets or country lanes without a signpost, stop, get out of your car and use the pendulum. Or, if you've been misdirected while walking in an unfamiliar town, you can use the pendulum to find major landmarks on foot. It's easier to use on foot, but even in a car or on a bicycle you can stop and dowse at every alternative route point.

Stop worrying about being late, panicking about being lost or cursing the stupidity of others for getting you in this mess, and concentrate on the problem. Look round and realise what a pleasant place you are in – there's no point in offending the resident local spirits. Explain to them that you need to get somewhere fast.

First establish two responses from your pendulum. Ask it to demonstrate the 'right way' and 'off-course' responses. The first might be a circling movement clockwise, the second anti-clockwise or cessation of movement, but you will discover a unique response. Let the key swing quite naturally. Then begin walking or ask a sympathetic passenger in the car to interpret the pendulum direction as he/she holds it en route.

Ask the pendulum to make a positive response in the correct direction. Each time you stop remark how nice the place is, and with any luck the local elves will hasten you in the right direction. If you see any litter en route pick it up, provided it's not too revolting; I carry a plastic bag for such times as I need to appease the earth in a hurry. Before you know it, you're at your destination.

Sometimes, however, we get lost not deliberately but because deep down we don't want to arrive. Our unconscious wisdom is warning us that maybe we might be happier elsewhere. In this case beneath our anxiety is a sense of relief that the decision is apparently out of our hands.

If arriving isn't vital, ask your pendulum if it is right for you to go to the place you're heading. If not, ask your pendulum to show you the right way. Many people have missed an appointment, lost their route and ended up meeting someone or going somewhere that has changed the course of their lives.

If you don't have any string, use a key, a piece of jewellery, a crystal or even a stone from the wayside, held lightly between the fingers of your left hand in a position that feels natural. In this case, the normal positive pendulum swing will be replaced by a strong vibration in your fingers when you are heading in the right direction.

PARKING HAZARDS

Though today we are free of highwaymen and roads full of potholes, modern frustrations can disturb the harmony of our journeying.

A parking spell

- It was Jane's first day at work after maternity leave, and there were no parking spaces in the car park that served several offices. They had all filled up while she was sitting fuming in a traffic jam caused by roadworks in the local town centre.

  Jane was running late. Just as she was leaving, the baby had been sick over the city suit she had stayed up till midnight ironing, and she knew that her elderly male office colleagues would have little sympathy.

Jane sat in her car and yelled at the unfairness of life. She needed to be on time, and need is the first requirement of magic. She was not being selfish. Successful magic is always needs-motivated, and not a party or ego trip. She selected the parking space in the car park she wanted, although she was prepared to compromise.

She noted the cars next to the vehicle in the chosen space, and paid special attention to the car that was going to move just for her. Jane admired its colour and make, and above all commented to herself what a very nice car it was and what a benign, discerning driver it must have to choose such a vehicle. Positivity is vital in magic; panicking or cursing wastes energy.

Jane went for a drive round the square to give the other driver time to decide to move and vacate the parking lot; parking near the chosen place in anticipation may reserve the space, but allows doubts to creep in. In her mind Jane visualised parking her own car in the now vacant place.

Jane thanked the driver who would vacate the space in advance and saw him or her driving off happily to somewhere exciting or fulfilling. Perhaps he was off for a suddenly remembered appointment (thanks to Jane's psychic promptings), or felt a spontaneous desire to make another person's mundane day rather special.

Sure enough, a sandy-haired businessman drove off in this car, chatting ten to the dozen on his mobile phone. Coincidence? Who cares? As Jane saw the chosen car disappearing round the corner, she remembered she owed the universe a favour. She vowed to pick someone who needed a bit of help or cheering up.

Try a parking spell. Wait until the occasion arises naturally, and don't invite the local press to attend. Real magic is a purely spontaneous experience in response to a real, immediate need. Demonstrating psychic abilities for gain is a very different ball game, and not a recommended way to increase personal harmony. The sheer anxiety involved in delivering magic, or for that matter mediumship, to order, can block natural intuitive and telekinetic powers and leave you or me looking a fraud or a fool. This is why so many psychic demonstrations on television programmes are usually nonstarters.

Save magic for when you or your loved ones need a boost; use it quietly, unobtrusively, and exchange stories with other sympathetic women who also have felt the call.

Your parking spell didn't work? You didn't believe it would. Don't worry; it took a long time to forget childhood magic, when anything was possible and Santa's grotto stretched all the way to the North Pole and didn't end at the shoe department of the big store. By the end of this book everyday magic will be so routine as to be automatic. The first time seems like a miracle, but as the psychologist Skinner found with the pigeons he taught to play ping-pong in the interests of science, reinforcement is the best way to strengthen certainty in your own natural powers.

Remember, however, that once you join the magic club, it's not a one-way street. If you get a buzzing in your head and feel a desire to move your car before time, maybe some other witch- or warlock-designate urgently needs help or your parking space. It won't take a minute. If it's not life and death, give someone else a helping hand. Now the cosmos owes you a favour. The cosmos is remarkably democratic, and the idea of psychic cash flow with credits and debits is not such a strange one.

Spells for traffic wardens and traffic police

We need traffic wardens and police to make things run smoothly and ensure fair play. This concept is one you will need to accept if you are to maintain the positive, welcoming attitude that is necessary for the success of traffic spells.

If you know you are late getting back to a meter or have parked in a forbidden zone with good cause, visualise a kindly, smiling representative of officialdom whose only aim is to keep things running smoothly, and is aware that human error can necessitate stretching rules for an urgent need. Smile at the distant figure hovering near your car as you hurry towards your vehicle. First bathe the official in a soft, pink, reconciliatory glow – use anything pink in the environment to get it going, or keep a pink crystal in your pocket for such an eventuality.

Secondly, divert his or her attention from your vehicle. This isn't affecting someone else's behaviour – that's off-limits. You are simply offering an alternative focus. Nor should you try negative magic; creating a traffic foul-up two blocks away would cause inconvenience to others.

What would make the warden happy and give him something interesting to watch instead of pavements and cars? How about an orderly procession, a circus with spangled acrobats and a couple of clowns? Jugglers? A carnival float on its way to an event, covered with flowers or flags. A traction engine steaming and whistling its way to a rally, towing a fairground organ playing those old songs we all love? How about a band, traditional, jazz, even a church group playing favourite hymns? And you sitting in the seat of your car pulling away from the kerb with a friendly smile and wave.

You could offer him or her an alternative venue. Taking care of traffic is hungry and thirsty work, so evoke some delicious cooking smells in your mind – hot dogs, pancakes, fresh bagels. An ice-cream van complete with chimes, selling delicious home-made chocolate ice cream, recalls childhood pleasures. Fresh percolating coffee – it must be time for a short break, for lunch, to finish the shift for the day.

Even if your friendly warden is heading off in the other direction don't be tempted to spin out your stay. It will cost you enough psychic points without going into double time.

A SPELL FOR TRAVELLING

Long-lost relations bearing a suitcase containing your inheritance in gold bars are rare. So are exotic holiday offers which come out of the blue – which don't carry strings longer than the rope to tie up the QE2.

However, if you've got a location in mind that is within your wildest dreams, or the possibility of a trip abroad, whether in connection with your job or a holiday, you can hurry things along and make yourself more receptive to a change of scene.

Pick a symbol for the means of transport, a toy plane, boat, train, car, or even a model bicycle if you fancy backpacking round the world. You can get paper flags of different countries or plastic ones from packs of toy soldiers, and if there's a particular country or continent you have in mind, place the flag next to your mode of transport. Find the rough direction of your journey, and point your transport in the direction you will travel from your home or workplace.

Ring the plane or other mode of transport with bright crystals, beads or buttons in red, orange, yellow and white to give energy to your plans. If you have a crystal wand or a clear crystal quartz, point the sharp, clear end in the direction you wish to travel, and see yourself propelled on a brilliant shaft of white light towards your destination. Feel the warmth, or the cold ice or the dust of the new place, whatever is an identifying feature, and look up at the sun, moon or clouds where you are now and see them in the new setting.

Leave the crystals and the plane pointing towards your destination for 24 hours, and do anything you can to advance your travel plans in the real world, even if it involves modifying your ideas, finding a way to raise the money, or developing your potential to make a travel offer more likely.

Collect brochure pictures or postcards of your chosen destination and place them under the crystal ring. If the project does not seem to be developing immediately, each morning on waking concentrate on your destination and repeat the spell when you feel your optimism wavering.

SPELLS FOR TICKETS

Whether you're on standby for Seattle or need to change your reservation for a coach ticket to Manchester, it is so frustrating to queue, only to be told as you reach the booth or check-in desk that the last ticket has just gone.

Don't despair; there are always one or two tickets that have been overlooked. A cancellation may be coming in at the moment you have been refused. You may have to be adaptable – an extra plane change at Dallas or an extra hour at Birmingham waiting for a coach connection.

All you need is to kindle the spirit of the chase in the huntress Diana or golden Apollo standing behind the airline desk or ticket booth. When the airline official or travel agent says 'No', pause and smile while you summon up your own positive feelings and sound the clarion from a golden horn that only they can hear.

Place the official on a white horse or golden chariot and let the elusive document or ticket flutter in the breeze in front of them, just out of touch. Look the person you are dealing with full in the eyes and remind them, telepathically, how much they enjoy a challenge, what a great person they are, how enterprising, and how they have never been defeated but always rise to the occasion. Let a cool breeze flow over them. If they feel hot and bothered, they may give up.

As they cautiously begin to flick through alternative routes on the computer screen, or rummage through the reserve tray of ticket, make encouraging noises, all the while letting them roam the cool green forest, their golden arrows darting through the thicket. With mounting excitement they leap over boulders and through bracken. The prey is within their grasp – and they come up with the ticket or alternative route. Thank them profusely and wish them a nice day. In return, vow in future to cancel any reservations you don't need as early as possible.

I tried this at Los Angeles International Airport the day of the earthquake in January 1994, when amidst the panic at the airport, I needed to bring my return flight forward by a day. I ended up flying back by a longer but incredibly picturesque route to England, and enjoying a brief stop-over in Seattle.

A CLEAR RUN

Not all travel is exotic. Getting from A to B via the dry cleaners, the bank and the supermarket, can cause more stress than crossing the Atlantic in Concorde. The following spell will easily adapt to any bottleneck in your day.

You've got ten minutes to get round the supermarket. Half the check-outs are closed, and the customers in front are counting out their piggy banks in pennies, or paying with credit cards from obscure banks that warrant a long-distance phone call for each transaction.

Positivity is the key, so don't stand with fingers drumming, foot tapping and smoke coming out of your ears. You might be able to contact an equally receptive person higher up the queue to let you slip in, but if not, decide what alternative entertainment you can provide so the queue clears to give you long enough to nip through.

Pick up an apple or other fruit or vegetable, or some grain-based product from your trolley as a symbol of plenty. Demeter or Ceres, goddesses of corn and plenty, represent the energies of abundance you need to transfer to the supermarket manager or manageress to get things moving. These enterprising people generally have a special offer up their sleeves to promote trade and goodwill. Reduced avocados, fresh pineapples, sliced bread are good triggers for this abundance factor, and satisfy humanity's need to forage or hunt for food. You're just harnessing this instinctive trend at an optimum time for you.

Judge the mood of the queue, whether they are secret grape fanciers or more the glazed cherry brigade, and convey this telepathically to the manager or manageress, along with a golden light to surround them and set in motion their personal abundance factor. Then visualise the queue rushing towards the centre aisle, where this absolutely unbeatable offer is taking place.

Hear the voice over the tannoy inviting the shoppers to snap up this bargain, and feel the touch of the rough pineapple leaves, the prickly avocados, the soft dough of the reduced loaf. Smile at the manager as they bask in the success of the brilliant timing of the offer, remembering not to be tempted to dash off and stock up yourself, thereby destroying the whole point of the enterprise.

MAGICAL ELEMENTAL JOURNEYS

In Chapter 4, I suggested elemental magic that can be practised in park or garden. A day out to the sea or country can also offer you contact with the ancient elements and give you space to allow your magical powers to come to the fore, unchecked by the demands of others or the everyday world.

Go alone or with a trusted friend. Find a quiet sandy shore for earth and water magic. A visit to an early morning beach or riverside, where the current will have imprinted images of its own on the sand or silt, will offer images for you to interpret in accordance with your symbol system. Go at sunrise or sunset on a windy day and see fire and air pictures scud across the sky. You may see one of your root images, or perhaps a picture or scene that evokes an idea or even words.

- Ellen desperately wanted a child, but her partner said that although he would continue to live with her if she became pregnant, she would have to use artificial insemination, and the baby would be hers alone.

Since she loved Bob she didn't want to make love with another man, and so she had to decide whether to try for a baby by artificial means or abandon the idea. She got up early and drove to a beach about 30 miles away.

Using a stick she found, she closed her eyes and randomly pushed the piles of wettish sand into a shape she felt was right. When she opened her eyes she saw a face formation. By coincidence, two stones were in the position of eyes. This face seemed sad and she saw this as her own.

Next to it, but quite separate, was a shape that looked like a baby's cradle, and some distance away was the shape of a lorry surrounded by hills of sand. Ellen realised that she had been hoping that if she became pregnant Bob would change his attitude and welcome the child as his own. This was a vain hope, however, and she saw the lorry as Bob's driving away. The sand wasn't foretelling a future that would come to pass out of the blue. The seeds were there, but the picture showed Ellen aspects she hadn't been acknowledging because they were so painful.

Why was the baby's cradle apart from her, and between her and the truck? It's easy but wrong to interpret other people's readings. I would have said that Ellen would bring up the child alone and that she didn't need Bob, but Ellen said the baby was driving a wedge between her and Bob, and she would resent the child for driving him away. Ellen decided to stick with Bob and try to forget the baby. She is very sad, and five years on doesn't know if she made the right decision.

Sand magic

Draw a circle with a stick or feather found on the beach and in it write the name of the person you want to be with, or the goal you have. Enclose it with your name written on pebbles, and let the tide carry your desires with it. If you want to get rid of something, write the name of the bad experience or feeling in the circle and rub it out, letting the tide erase the empty circle.

Sand divination

Take a pile of sand, close your eyes and swirl it with a stick from the beach. You will see when you open your eyes that you've made a shape or even a picture. Let the first image or words that come into your head, however unlikely, provide the answer.

You may find familiar images or a whole scene. Let your intuition guide you as to the meaning. The Ancient Egyptians were devotees of sand divination, while Jung believed that sand therapy, using small figures, could unlock the secrets of a mind's conflicts. You could place one or two of your magical symbols in the picture you have created, and see what the scene suggests.

Magic sandcastles

Make two sand or stone castles next to one another, close to the shore. Designate one 'Yes' and one 'No', or two different options. The one the sea takes first will be the right answer. If they disappear together then neither option is right, and if it's a 'Yes'/'No' you're not asking the right question.

The tides

We may no longer go to the lengths of fishermen in the Western Isles of Scotland, where at Hallowe'en a fisherman wades into the sea with a cup of ale as a sacrifice for the sea god. However, the tide is a powerful impetus for magic.

The incoming tide – can be used to herald new beginnings. Write on a stone with another pebble what it is you want to begin, whether a relationship, a new job or even a new approach to a problem. Throw them as hard as you can and see yourself taking that first step towards happiness or success. These things won't come for free, and having used the sea magic you then have to make them happen by your own effort.

The turning tide – harnesses the full power of the sea and should be used when you need to make a tremendous leap in your life, or when you have taken the first steps in a new venture or relationship but don't seem to be getting anywhere. As the tide turns, throw a symbol of what you desire on to the waves as they reach the shore – fruit for fertility, a coin for wealth, flowers for love, a toy boat for travel, a key for a new home, an old car key (not your only set!) for a new car, or the name of your loved one carved on a stone. As you do so see yourself in the desired situation as you are now, not two stone lighter or more beautiful.

The outgoing tide – is for 'kicking' bad habits or redundant relationships (you can't heave unwanted lovers wearing concrete boots into the water). Cast a stone bearing the name of the habit or relationship you want to offload, seeing the old ties going out with the tide. Repeat the magic if your resolve weakens.

In all personal divination the images are personal and so sceptics can argue that you see what you want. However, often two different forms of divination give the same result, and in the vast majority of cases the advice given is sound. Whether the choice is being influenced by unconscious wishes – and it's the unconscious wisdom we are seeking – or by some more magical processes, the result is positive, and often goes against the more obvious, but erroneous solution.

Light a small fire on the shoreline. Draw a circle in the sand around the fire and within it, in tiny black pebbles, etch the words, 'Forgive', 'Succeed', 'Love' – whatever the urgent need is in your life.

Take off your shoes and slowly move around the fire, creating spiralling footprints in the sand and stamping the circle into the earth. As you pass on the sea side, kick away the encroaching water. As the tide comes in, dance in the shallows until the words are erased by the waves and the fire fades from existence.

If you can find any sea flowers or plants growing on sand dunes or wooded slopes, sea lavender, for example, cast them into the sea as an offering. Stand barefoot in the shallows and reach into the water as each wave comes. On the second or third wave, you will be offered a sea treasure, perhaps a holey stone, sacred to the old sea deities, or a special piece of quartz. Carry it or wear it, and absorb its wisdom.

GETTING IN TOUCH
WITH THE SEASONS

From the beginning of human consciousness, the sun and moon have been central to the lives of mankind, not only for warmth, light and marking the passage of times and the seasons, but as symbols of man's own inner powers.

The sun, masculine, powerful, courageous, assertive, speaks of our conscious strength to succeed, and directs our energies in a linear way. It corresponds to *yang*, to the left-brain, to light, convergent thinking and to creativity. The moon, feminine, mysterious, intuitive, nurturing, is the *yin* power, dark, unconscious, the right side of the brain, divergent thinking, equally powerful but operating in cycles of time.

It is wrongly assumed that magic uses only the right side of the brain involving intuition and unconscious powers. That is only half the story. The magic of the Aztecs, Greeks, Egyptians, Chinese, Celts and the alchemists who sought to combine the essence of King Sol with Queen Luna, recognised the need for powerful, direct energy and action, as well as intuitive powers.

By harnessing the power of the sun as well as the moon, left-brain, logical magic does not usurp, but supplements the mystique of lunar powers. As well as recognising the cyclic nature of human lives and lunar magic, solar magic can use the A to Z surge of direct energy to propel its energy into real action.

Women have within them energies that correspond to both the sun and the moon, and the power of the sun can give to women the focused energy to turn dreams into reality, plans into action.

SOLAR OR LUNAR MAGIC?

Solar power is best for matters in the conscious, outer world, and for material matters, family matters, a better job, money or establishing a strong identity.

Things of the spirit, inner issues and emotions, spells for love and kicking deep-seated habits or destructive relationships, are better in moonlight, where the unconscious powers predominate. You'll know instinctively if it's a solar or lunar issue, and whether you need a blast of sun power for clarity, or more subtle moon bindings or unravellings. Sunday, Sol's day, the day of the sun, is good for solar spells, while Monday for Mani, the moon goddess of the north, is harmonious for moon spells.

THE TIMING OF SPELLS

With solar magic, if it's a new beginning, go for dawn. For full power or realising your potential do your magic at noon, and for banishing spells, try sunset. If it's a vital issue, you could go from sunrise to sunset, with your most powerful energies at noon.

The moon with its phases is a slower magic, and goes from A to Z and back to A again. Many women find the cyclic nature of moon magic fits in well with their own ebbs and flows, but you might not want to wait for 20 or so days for the right bit of the cycle to occur. You may find it easier to divide moon spells into three, the first for a new beginning or relationship on the new and waxing (increasing) moon, the full moon for bringing plans to fruition or using your full female power. The waning and dark of the moon, those last days when we trust the new moon is in the sky, are ideal for ending relationships or letting go of redundant stages in your life.

COMBINING THE POWERS

For important issues you can combine the power of the sun and moon. For example, for a new beginning, you could begin your spell at dawn on the first day of the new moon or during the waxing moon period; for full power you would wait until the first day of the full moon or any time during the week of the full moon, and carry out your spell at noon.

For a powerful ending you would wait until the week of the waning moon, especially the last days of the old moon, that time when we cannot see it in the sky. Look in the weather section in your newspaper if you are uncertain of the current moon phase, but use your intuitive feel for when the moon phase is right. Carry out your spell at sunset.

A JOINT SOLAR/LUNAR
SPELL FOR MOVING HOUSE

Buying a house

You can try this spell at dawn during the new moon period, so that both solar and lunar powers operate and an initial surge of energy is supported by the slower moon time, which brings intuitive processes into play as well as the logical skills of the sun potency.

Finding a house that feels right at an affordable price in a suitable location needs luck, application, perseverance – and a little magic. Use a model house, perhaps one from a Monopoly set, a toy or china house, or even a picture. If you use a picture or photograph of a desirable dwelling choose one that is roughly the size and kind you would like to buy. Full colour illustrations of Buckingham Palace are unlikely to result in a sudden elevation of fortunes.

Place the model house on a road map in approximately the area of your chosen move. If you aren't tied to a particular region, take a chance, revolve the map nine or ten times clockwise and put the house down without looking. An unlikely change of location may prove not only possible but an improvement in your life.

Place the key of your present home underneath the model house, and see yourself closing the door of your old home for the very last time and pushing the key through the letterbox.

Now visualise yourself driving or travelling by train to the new house. Picture it in your mind's eye, and you will be surprised when you come across your new home for the first time how close it is to your inner picture. Pick out one identifying feature, a magnolia bush in the front garden, a cracked pane in the front door, or a front door with a lion knocker. See a shiny new key opening the door and feel the roughness of the door-mat and the house not empty, but full of your furniture and treasures.

To the north of the model house place a small piece of brick, to represent the bricks and mortar of the house. To the east of the house put a clothes peg, to represent washing drying in the air in your new garden or on your balcony. To the south, place a box of matches to represent warmth or cooking in your new home, and to the west, a bath or sink plug to symbolise the water in your new home. You may think of more appropriate symbols for your own earth, air, fire and water domestic symbols. As you place each one, visualise yourself inside your home, cooking or washing up, engaged in deliberately mundane activities, as this is a spell for bricks and mortar and so needs a physical bias.

Place the map, the model house and the symbols on your window ledge and leave them there until the full moon period is ending. You may dream of your house and get further clues as to its location. Mark the place on the map with a cross, and go and find it, or something very similar. In reality, you'll find you know the twists and turns of the roads leading to it, if you trust your instinct.

Selling a house

This is a spell to be done at dusk at any period during the time of the waning moon. Somewhere is the person for whom your home is perfect, who will see the faults of your present residence as appealing eccentricities, and appreciate its subtle charms. I always seem to sell to DIY enthusiasts, so my own domestic ineptitude must serve a purpose in the wider scheme. Picture your home's most attractive and unique features, whether the garden, an unusual entrance, or the view from the top floor. Even houses on apparently standardised estates have unique features if you can locate them.

Again use your model house on a map, but this time rest the key on top of it because you want someone to pick up the key. Potential buyers can come from anywhere. Scatter nails at random over the map. Hold a magnet over your model house and revolve it until you have gathered a number of nails. As you do this visualise different groups of people coming to view your home. Let them sniff appreciatively the aroma of fresh coffee and the vase of red (for action) flowers you have put in the entrance. This psychological ploy will act as an immediate psychic trigger when the buyers come in actuality, and you (and maybe they) relive the moment. You may even sell to another witch who tried the moving spell. Mentally focus on the unique feature of your home, and be glad you can make these visitors happy by letting them buy it.

Place the map, key, nails and magnet, and model house on your window ledge as the moon begins to wane; once the new moon appears in the sky your buyers should come. You can run this and the previous spell throughout the whole monthly cycle, concentrating on the dawn and dusk solar periods to give continuing impetus. Try for several months, each time extending the area and number of your nails, and pointing out other attractive features of your house in your visualisation.

SEASONAL MAGIC

The sun and moon were closely allied with eight ancient festivals that divided the agricultural year, and which are reflected today in many of our modern celebrations. Around these periods, certain issues have strong affinities, for example money magic about Christmas, but when you need a money spell you can call on the midwinter powers, perhaps by adding incense or herbs of that period. The festivals alternate solar/lunar, beginning with the solar midwinter solstice. The dates of the solar festivals, the solstices and equinoxes, can vary slightly, so check them on your calendar. In Celtic times festivals, like days, ran from sunset to sunset and would last for three days, so began on the eve of what we would regard as the actual day, hence Hallowe'en.

General sun herbs and incense include acacia, bay, carnation, cedarwood, celandine, camomile, cinnamon, frankincense, juniper, mistletoe, saffron, St John's wort, rosemary and rue.

General moon herbs and incense include dog rose, gardenia, jasmine, ginger, iris, lemon and lemon balm, myrrh, sandalwood, poppy seed and wallflower.

These can be used in any of your lunar or solar spells as incense or fragrances, or you can even use the actual herbs as part of your earth element.

MIDWINTER: FOR MONEY
AND PRACTICALITIES

Midwinter solstice magic, the period around 21 December, is the time for spells for money or practical benefits. Christmas is and has been, albeit under different names in other times and cultures, a time when the midwinter gloom demands on a primitive level that we counter the darkness of cold, short days and long nights with a celebration of light and life and hope of a better future.

Our present festival is a glorious amalgamation and compromise of many ancient festivals that centred around the midwinter solstice, Norse, Celtic, Mithraic, Greek and Roman, as well as Christian celebrations. The common theme is that the sun (or Son of God) is reborn at the darkest hour of the year, and life begins again. The vegetation will grow once more, the sun will give longer and warmer days, and we've got a new chance of getting it right.

The best time of year for money spells

Mid-December and January, especially around the midwinter solstice, but you can do the spells at any time, using evergreen leaves or boughs or midwinter incense and herbs, which include cedar, feverfew, pine and rosemary.

A solar money spell

We've all turned silver coins over to the new moon in the hope that this will increase our fortunes. Yet we know that no magician or clairvoyant can produce that crock of gold or spin gold from straw, and any offers of instant cash from whatever source should be viewed with caution. There's generally a 'pay back with interest clause', whether in monetary or personal terms.

Modern money spells rely more on galvanising our own capacity to generate money, and sometimes this power in us needs kick-starting into action in the real world. So the solar power at dawn can be a good time for a new financial beginning, or at noon if you've already taken the first steps and need a boost. To get yourself out of debt, wait until the sun is a big red ball at sunset. You can, of course, carry out the spell during the new moon period for additional growing power.

Find a place where the sun is shining into a series of puddles after rain, into rockpools, or forming a golden path across a river, canal or the sea. Because money is associated with the earth element but you are harnessing the power of the sun, use a series of shiny pennies, brass discs or even gold-coloured buttons, nine in number, and recite nine times, faster and faster: 'Sun be sunny, bring me money.'

Drop or cast the first golden symbol into the water close to you, repeat the rhyme another nine times, dropping another coin slightly further away, and so on until you have thrown the nine coins into the path of light or the sun's image. Make your final cry loud, and fling the ninth coin as far as you can.

If you are using puddles or rockpools, you can jump from one to the other, dropping a coin after each nine chants.

VALENTINE'S DAY:
FOR LOVE

Brigantia/Valentine's Day for new romance and relationships, is one of the lunar festivals. You may choose to keep to the traditional Celtic dates for Imbolc or Brigantia, the festival of ewes' milk, from 31 January to 2 February, which I mentioned in Chapter 1. Or you may wish to practise love magic around St Valentine's Eve or Day on 14 February, which was also the day, according to Chaucer, when the birds chose a mate.

St Valentine was a young priest who defied an edict of the Emperor Claudius that soldiers should not be allowed to marry, as it made them poor fighters. St Valentine conducted the weddings of a number of young soldiers, and was executed on 14 February, AD 269, thereafter becoming the patron saint of lovers. It is said that while he was in prison he restored the sight of the gaoler's blind daughter, who fell in love with him.

The love and fertility associations with 14 February were also an offshoot of the ancient Roman festival, Lupercalia, held a day later, on the spot where Romulus and Remus were suckled by the wolf. The horned god, in the form of the Lycean nature deity, Pan, put in an appearance, as he offered protection to the flocks from wolves. Lupercalia was primarily a festival of youth; Lupercus was the Roman version of Pan.

The best time of year for love spells

February to mid-March, but you can do love spells at any time of the year, using a circle of candles and a container of fresh milk, or the incense and herbs of Brigantia, which include angelica, basil, celandine and myrrh.

A lunar love spell

For furthering a new relationship, whether love or friendship, you can carry out this spell, or your own, when the crescent moon first appears in the sky. If possible find a sheltered place close to water, perhaps by a river. A grove of silver birch trees, silver being the colour of the moon, would be perfect, but you can equally well use your garden pond or even a sink of water.

Find something made of copper, the metal of Venus, classical goddess of love. Copper is believed to attract love or friendship. Mimosa, Venus's sacred herb, was once set in copper rings, so if you can add mimosa so much the better. As well as the herbs of Brigantia, there are those herbs and flowers sacred to love; myrtle, also sacred to Venus, is another good addition, or jasmine, the flower and incense of the moon. The rose is both flower and incense of Venus. Failing that, use any natural flower or herb that is special to you. Maybe your love gave you a bizzy lizzie plant – if that's your love symbol, use it.

We can't make people love us. Nor should we, but we can make our own loving energies especially potent and send them in the direction of the object of our affections. Sending out a general call to be loved is a shot in the dark; there are no guarantees as to who you will end up with.

Make a green ray of light come from your heart and direct it wherever you know your love is. As you use it to transmit your powerful loving energies, whisper softly the name of the person you have affection for, and see your lover opening his or her arms to receive the love, and magnifying it back. Now turn your piece of copper over at the new moon, as you do with money, and ask in your own words that as the moon increases so will the love symbolised by the copper.

Take a small tray of earth and bury your copper object in it, or sow fast-growing seeds in the shape of your lover's first initial. If your love is meant to be, by the time they have grown your relationship will develop and thrive.

CELANDINE

EASTER: FOR NEW BEGINNINGS

Easter/the spring equinox, is a solar festival for new beginnings, whether a new career or a determination to assert your own independence and identity.

Wake at dawn on Easter Sunday and you can see the sun play and dance for joy. Hurry to a stream or river – you've only got a few minutes – for in the reflected rays you'll see angels frolicking in the water.

We think of Easter as purely a Christian feast, and for many of us it is a very special time of the year. As with all Christian festivals, however, Easter celebrations began with man's earliest awareness of the seasons, and even today mark a time of growth and rebirth after the darkness of winter. In pagan days the vernal or spring equinox was a tribute to the goddess of spring, Ostara or Eastre.

Indeed, the vernal equinox or Ostara Time, 21-23 March, marks the transition point between the dark and light halves of the year. At the spring equinox, the sun rises due east and sets due west, giving exactly 12 hours of daylight, and in Christianity the resurrection of Christ is associated with the restoration of light to the world. Though the moon plays no part at any other time of the Christian year, Easter Sunday falls between 21 March and 25 April. It is regulated by the paschal moon, and falls on the first Sunday following the full moon after the vernal equinox.

The best time of year for new beginnings magic

From mid-March to the end of April, but you can do your new beginnings spells at any time, using a branch from a birch tree, the tree of regeneration, or a growing pot of seeds. The incense and herbs of the spring equinox include celandine, cinquefoil, honeysuckle, jasmine, iris and thyme.

A solar spell for a new path

This spell is best done at noon, perhaps at the period of the full moon, to harness both lunar and solar powers, which represent the conscious and unconscious powers within you. This will enable you to reach your full potential in whatever field you choose. It's important for you to decide the path you wish to follow, whether you are aiming for the top, or are happier using your creative and practical skills to make your own particular sun shine.

Make a yellow paper disc to represent the sun. In the centre make a large dark dot. This is the ancient astrological sign for the sun. On that dot place a lighted candle, which may be coloured red for energy, orange for self-confidence or yellow for clear communication. Now write on a piece of red, yellow or orange paper your first desire or goal. You may be surprised at this, as the values and opinions of others may have guided you on to a path that is right for them but not for you. Fold the paper and consign it to the flame, all the while chanting softly, 'I am choosing the path that is right for me', until it has disappeared. Put your candle in a safe place and let its flame burn down naturally. Carve the old sign for the sun in the melted wax, when it has set, and keep this on your window ledge until the moon begins to wane.

If it's a sunny day, you may prefer to use a circular mirror reflecting the sun's rays to start a small fire, and burn your wish on this.

MAY DAY: FOR FERTILITY

Beltane/May Day, is a lunar festival for fertility, whether in growing love, a business venture bearing fruit, or conceiving a child.

On the eve of 30 April, May revels celebrate the coming of the Celtic summer, Beltane. This was the time when the cattle were let out of the barns and driven between twin fires to purify them. Bel or Belenos was the old sun god. His head, or that of a king named after him, is said to be buried under Tower Hill in London.

Young men would leap over the fires with the girls with whom they had spent the night, looking for the first may (hawthorn) blossoms to decorate the houses. A Beltane cake was baked and divided into portions. It was placed in a bag, and the person who picked out the piece marked with the cross was the mock, and in ancient times the real, sacrifice.

The maypole was a symbol of ancient tree worship, and symbolised one of the old world trees, such as the Norse Yggdrasil. Maypole dances involved winding red and blue, green, yellow and white ribbons, representing the union of earth and sky, winter and summer, water and fire, in spiralling shapes, to represent the spiralling earth energies. The May Queen was the final appearance of the maiden aspect of the goddess before she became the mother goddess, and so Maytime is associated with fertility.

The best time of year for fertility magic

May to mid-June, but you can practise fertility spells at any time, using a crystalline egg or an egg-shell split in half. The incense and herbs of Beltane include almond, angelica, frankincense, lilac and meadowsweet.

A lunar fertility spell

Whether for a child, a new project to take root, or a new relationship to bear fruit, this spell begins on the new moon and continues until the full moon is in the sky.

Use either a crystalline egg, such as the dragon's egg, or two matching agate geodes that can be bought for a few pounds from a good New Age shop or mineral centre. Make sure the top and bottom fit together and leave a hollow inside. You can even use an ordinary empty egg-shell dyed in a gentle colour such as pink or green.

This represents the cosmic egg from which all life came, and indeed Easter eggs are a powerful fertility symbol – good news for chocaholics. Inside the shell, place a tiny moonstone, or a tiny doll if you are eager to conceive a child, and put the egg on the window ledge at the beginning of the moon cycle. Open the egg and let any moonlight shine on the moonstone, but close it during the day.

When it is the first day of the full moon, insert a sharp needle into the egg-shell or within the crystal egg, and leave in the moonlight.

Next morning wrap the needle and moonstone in a special shawl or scarf and keep it in a drawer until the next new moon. If it is a career matter, make positive efforts from the first day of the full moon to bring your ideas to fruition.

If you are trying to conceive a child, begin the spell on the first day of your menstrual cycle, and insert the needle in the egg when you are around ovulation; you may be using a thermometer or know from the mid-cycle pain and restlessness some women feel that this is the right time. You can repeat this spell over several months.

THE LONGEST DAY:
FOR SUCCESS, POWER AND HEALTH

The summer solstice or longest day, for success, power and health, is a solar festival held around 21 June.

It marks the height of the power of the solar deity, whose

festival has been celebrated in different cultures; the Persian Mithras, Balder in the Norse tradition, and Belenos of the Celts. From Russia in the north to Greece and Rome in the south, the summer solstice was an important festival from early times, as man tried, by sympathetic magic, to hold the sun's power and stop its decline.

At midsummer, the longest day, there was an ancient tradition of lighting bonfires on beacon hills to celebrate the power of the sun, which had reached its height, and to try to persuade the sun to remain high in the sky and not to wane and bring longer nights and colder days. The effect of many hilltop bonfires was believed to strengthen the power of the sun. The Aryans believed they were actually giving it fire. Fire wheels were rolled down the hillsides, flaming tar barrels swung on chains, and blazing torches tossed in the air. The higher you jumped over the bonfire the higher the corn would grow, and if you got over without being singed you would be married within the year!

Fields were circled sunwise with processions of flaming torches to bless them, and the woman chosen as Earth Mother would cast a bonfire of flowers and herbs, tied with red and blue, green, yellow and white ribbons, on to the hilltop fire, representing the union of earth and sky, winter and summer, water and fire.

The best time of year for a solstice empowerment spell

Mid-June to the end of July, but it can be carried out at any time, using yellow flowers or an oak twig as a focus. The herbs and incense of the summer solstice include cinquefoil, fennel, lavender, St John's wort and verbena.

A solar empowerment spell

Rise before dawn and build a small circle of stones, large enough to stand in, either in your garden or by a river.

Carry an oak twig, the tree king of the waxing (increasing) year. As the sun rises, circle the stone sunwise and burn your oak twig in the centre. Recite as you do so:

'Trefoil, vervain, John's wort, dill, let light and joy my darkness fill,
Trefoil, vervain, John's wort, thyme, let success and power be mine,
Trefoil, vervain, John's wort, fern, let my confidence return.'

If you can, spend the day outdoors, and just before sunset find a holly leaf (tree king of the waning year), circle your stones anti-clockwise and burn your holly twig or leaf in the centre, chanting:

'Trefoil, vervain, John's wort, dill, let power grow within me still,
Trefoil, vervain, John's wort, thyme, may good health and strength be mine,
Trefoil, vervain, John's wort, fern, grant my fortunes henceforth turn.'

LAMMAS: FOR JUSTICE

Lammas or Lughnassdadh is the festival of the first harvest, held in Celtic times from the eve of 31 July. It is a lunar festival, and powerful for magic concerning justice, rights and partnerships.

Lammas marked the beginning of autumn, and was a celebration of the Celtic god of wisdom and light, Lugh. As well as the harvesting of the corn, it involved the baking of the first loaf, hence the name 'Loaf-Mass'. Like many pagan festivals, it was taken over as Lammas-tide in the Church calendar.

The last sheaf to be cut, representing the slain corn god, was made into a corn dolly, symbol of the Earth Mother, and decorated with the scarlet ribbons of Frigg, the Norse mother goddess. The corn dolly would be hung over the hearth throughout the winter.

Because it was a time for feasting and meeting for the tribe, Lammas was traditionally a time for arranging marriages. Trial marriages, too, for a year and a day, were frequently set up at Lammas. The young couple would thrust their hands through a holed stone and agree to part after the designated period if either became disenchanted. Contracts in law were also fixed at this time, and the old name for the month in the Coligny calendar was Claim-time. This meant the Celtic debt collector would be round, as the roads were good enough to travel.

The best time of year for Lammas justice magic

From the end of July until mid-September, but you can perform it at any time, using a straw object such as a corn dolly, or any cereals. The herbs and incense of Lammas include aloes, cyclamen, frankincense, heather and myrtle.

A lunar justice spell

This is a spell for the waning moon period, to untangle disputes and clear the way ahead to resolve the matter. If there is an issue in which you have been treated unfairly, or you have strong principles about a matter and are being pressurised to compromise, make a circle of hazel sticks or hazelnuts, from the traditional tree of wisdom. The Vikings surrounded their judicial gatherings with hazel staves to mark its limits.

In the centre place a symbol of the matter under question – a coin for money matters, a document for legal affairs, a toy car if the dispute concerns a car, a toy house if there is property involved. Find something made of tin or bronze, the metal of Jupiter, the deity and planet representative of justice – a can of food with the label removed will do.

Wrap your symbol and the tin or bronze object in aluminium foil for the clear communication of Mercury; as you do so see all the unfairness and your own resentments bound tightly. Tie the parcel with string, and as you knot the string, tie up all the tangled arguments and disputes.

Leave the parcel on your window ledge until you first see the crescent moon in the sky. Take your parcel outside, and as you cut the cord see all the negative energies transformed into positive ones, freeing you for a new beginning. Make a positive wish on the new moon and try a new approach to your problem.

THE AUTUMN EQUINOX: FOR COMPLETION

The autumn equinox is for a final effort to tie up loose ends and finish tasks that are taking too long, or relationships that are no longer satisfying.

This solar festival, which took place in Celtic times about 21 September, was the time of equal day and night, the second harvest of vegetables and fruit, that is today celebrated in the Christian harvest festivals. Traditionally a time for harvest suppers, when the final harvest was gathered in, it represents the beginning of the darker nights and colder days, a time for looking backwards on what has been achieved, and completing tasks before the long winter.

The best time of year for equinox completion magic

Between the middle of September and the end of October, but it can be practised at any time using dried corn or grasses or a ripe apple as a symbol. Autumn equinox herbs and incense include ferns, geranium, honeysuckle, myrrh and sage.

A solar completion spell

Carry out this spell at dusk. Set an egg-timer for three minutes, until the sand runs through. Draw clockwise round the edges of a square box, instead of a circle, to denote limitation. Take a ball of black twine and slowly begin to bind the box, seeing as you do so the end come nearer, and chant, 'I am moving towards completion.'

Visualise the task to complete and the steps you will take, one after the other. Do not pause to deliberate or doubt; keep winding until your thread is wrapped round.

If you wind all the ball before the egg-timer is run through, loop the end and wait, seeing the effort being replaced by the satisfaction of completion. If the egg-timer finishes first, loop the twine just once and leave it, accepting that sometimes we have to acknowledge that there is only finite time and energy before we can move on.

Trace the line you drew anti-clockwise. Place the box in a closed cupboard and leave it. Make steps towards finishing the actual task.

HALLOWE'EN: FOR BANISHING

Hallowe'en or Samhain is for laying old ghosts, psychological as well as psychic. It was a major lunar festival.

Hallowe'en heralds the coldness and barrenness of winter and marks the beginning of the Celtic new year. It was the time when cattle were brought from the hills for the winter, and either put in byres or slaughtered for meat.

Hence with the new year connotations the gates of the year are said to open on to both the past and future. Hallowe'en is traditionally a time of divination.

In the Christian church the name 'All Souls' thinly disguises the ancient festival of the Day of the Dead, which is still practised in some Catholic countries today. It was believed in Celtic times that with the onset of winter the ghosts of the departed would come shivering from the woodlands and bare fields for the shelter of their former cottages. Food would be left in the kitchens or parlours for them to eat. It was believed that people should not go hunting on this day or the next, for fear of accidentally wounding a soul wandering about. In some Catholic countries flowers are laid from the cemetery to the house of the departed relative, and their favourite foods prepared.

The best time of year for banishing magic

November until the middle of December, but you can practise it any time, using the branch of a yew tree or a pine cone. The herbs and incense of Samhain include coriander, chives, cypress, dittany and tarragon.

A spell for banishing unwanted shadows of the past

Carry out this spell at the end of the old moon cycle, just before dusk. Go to a fast-flowing river with a flower of endings, such as Michaelmas daisy or gladioli, or any purple or dark blue flower. Sit on the bank and watch the light fade.

Let your regrets, sorrow and sadness pour in a dark band of light from your soul into the flower, reliving for the last time the harsh words, the painful loss. As the light leaves the sky or the sun sinks, cast your flower into the water and watch as it carries the sorrow away.

Plant seeds or a small stone at the spot where you threw the flower into the water. When you return home, take the first step towards that new beginning, even if it is only writing a declaration of intent in your diary.

STONE AND
CRYSTAL MAGIC

Stone magic is often neglected in favour of its more glamorous sister, crystal magic. Yet the contents of any garden can be used for inspiration and for harnessing natural energies.

MAKING A STONE CIRCLE OUTDOORS

A circle is considered magical because it has no beginning or end. Stone circles have had magical associations from early times, and it is believed that many of the old sites, such as Stonehenge, contain a wealth of astronomical wisdom that became lost with the demise of the Druids.

It's easy to make a stone circle in your garden, or in a park in the early morning before anyone is about. The stones need not be more than a few inches high, and you can have a raised, flat stone in the middle for your working place. A rockery can be easily adapted. A few herbs, especially those traditionally sacred to the sun, such as rosemary and bay, will add fragrance to your circle.

A day at the seaside or to a river in a local country park can also provide the material and setting for a circle. When you go somewhere special bring back a stone for your circle, and the memories of happy times will add to its positive powers.

A stone circle spell

If you have suffered a set-back or come to the end of a phase in your life it can be helpful to use stone circle magic to lay the foundations for a surer future. This is early morning magic, beginning either on the first day of a new month or in a new moon period. You can either make a stone pile, or a stone border along a flowerbed or even round a window box.

Plant seeds of hope, such as the lesser celandine for re-awakening of feeling, crocus for new beginnings, daisies for hope, feverfew for protection, primroses for new trust, rosemary for remembrance, in this case of past successes and strengths, and violets for small steps. If you live in more exotic climes you can plant any fruit seeds or even a flowering cactus.

Whether you go for a traditional triangular cairn of stones, a stone circle, a path or simple pile, the power of stones is the same.

Each day place a stone, and plant a few seeds or a stone from a fruit beside it. See the power of the rising sun, as representative of the fire element, warming and giving energy to your new endeavour, and make each stone signify a step, however small, towards your future. When doubts creep in, walk your stone path or border. Touch each of the stones and recall how far you have travelled. Go out in the wind and the rain and see air and water adding their power to your endeavours. If a stone falls, replace it and feel the confidence of your rebuilding.

Before long you may see the first shoots peeping through the ground. The stones are a reminder that nothing worthwhile comes overnight, and that whether you are developing your own inner world, establishing a new relationship, career or leisure interest, each step forward is an achievement, obstacles can be overcome and your new goal has sure foundations.

- Joanna wanted to leave her partner Paul, who had hit her several times and insisted that life was run according to his own rigid routine.

Over the years, Joanna had become afraid of being alone, and Paul had sapped her confidence. Anyone who vows that he or she would never be undermined by a partner has either been incredibly lucky or perhaps has never been in a position of financial or emotional vulnerability. Even the most successful women can lose confidence to survive alone in a relationship that means a lot to them. But such dependency is not set in stone. It just needs courage and maybe a little magic to gain confidence and self-love.

Joanna needed fire for inspiration, air for courage and logic, and the earth to remind herself of her own common sense and strength. So day by day, in a corner of the garden behind the shed, she began a circle of stones. Each day she placed a stone clockwise, and her determination to leave grew stronger as she paced around the circle, seeing herself walking away from the destructive situation into the light. On the day the circle was completed, she decided to leave.

Joanna went into Paul's regimented garden containing the pond he aerated with a fountain for exactly 30 seconds twice a day. She had found his obsessiveness endearing when they had lived separately, and thought it was just part of his funny bachelor ways. Five years of smoothing creases out of the newspaper and wiping round the jam pot before use to avoid a violent outburst, and she was no longer smiling indulgently.

Joanna took the stone she had placed in the centre of the circle and scratched on it, not Paul's name but her desire to be free. It was autumn and she threw the neatly swept pile of leaves into the air and stood tossing them on their way as they swirled around her. Now for the fire. She set fire to the pile of dead wood Paul had cut from a tree that was overhanging his patio, and finally threw her stone into his well-ordered pond, consigning her future to the flow of the water. For good measure she let the fountain bubble over her stone for several minutes, watching the water. She liberated the garden and her own nature.

Joanna packed a few essentials, for she knew Paul would haggle over the division of the spoils, and went to stay with a good friend at the other end of the country until she felt able to face the battle she knew she would inevitably have to extract any of the money she had put into the house. It's a romantic idea walking away for ever with just the clothes we stand up in, but like many of us, Joanna needed some money to begin her new life.

Magic offers no easy answers, but it can be the first step to a major change, and in the act of making our psychic gesture, spell, appeal to the universe, call it what you wish, we can ignite forces in ourselves that may find echoes in the benign energies all around us.

When I left a very unhappy set-up, I made a bonfire and burned all the things I no longer wanted or couldn't take with me, and as the sparks rose into the sky the rain fell and covered the garden momentarily with smoke and ashes. Damping down the fire, I left.

TALKING STONES

The ancient oracles of the classical period used the sound of water as it rushed over stones, usually out of some underground channel. Talking stones are a tradition that has largely died out, but it is a powerful form of divination in which you ask a question and listen to the answer in the water.

You may find a stream of rushing water or listen to the sea

on a shingle beach. If not, use your garden fountain or a cold tap or hose running over a bowl or bucket of stones.

You could begin by asking your stone oracle a question; before long you will tune into its voice and hear the answer. Once you feel in tune with the voice of earth and water, you can go on to use the stones and water as a focus for your personal spells.

WISHING WELL MAGIC

This is another form of stone and water magic, harnessing sound and water. Wells, especially holy ones, have always had magical significance, for here traditionally reside water spirits, whose favours can be bought by dropping coins.

Many of the old pagan wells which gave holy water were re-dedicated to Christian saints, and the custom of leaving money for the holy water became transposed into the idea of dropping coins into the well in return for prayers or wishes. The Romans even engraved curses on lead tablets and dropped them into the waters of Sulis Minerva at the Roman Baths in Bath. As a coin hits the water, so the sound sends the wish into the cosmos.

Well dressing, leaving flowers or tying ribbons or rags to local trees, is still practised in Wales, Cornwall, Ireland and the north of England in springtime. I found rags tied to the trees near the urban well I found in Bristol.

If you cannot find a well – and a place name is often a good clue – you can drop marked stones or coins into your garden pond, which you can ring with special stones to add to the earth magic. But the magic still works if you use a bucket of water.

Find a small stone close to the well or pond or other source of water, such as a lake in a park. With another sharp stone, carve on this stone a letter or symbol of whatever it is you want. As you hold your stone over the well or water, see yourself as the person you are now in a happier situation, and hear the sound of the water in your mind increase from the single sound of the stone, to a rushing river and finally to the sea.

Let the stone fall, and wait until you hear the sound of it reaching the water. If it is faint, then you know your stone has already travelled far. Leave a flower by the well or pond in thanks, and tie a ribbon or scarf to the nearest tree. If someone else picks it up and gives it to a friend or loved one, you have helped the spread of happiness.

ATTRACTING SPELLS

Find two matching stones, the first to represent your unchanging self and the second to stand for your need. These spells can be carried out at dawn, or when you see the crescent moon in the sky, or during the new moon period. The first day of the month is also a good choice. If you are using a tidal river or the sea, find out the time the tide turns from any tide-table, and use that to add to the initial impetus. But you can do the spell in a pond or even a bucket of water.

Using the stone of self, scratch the name of the person you wish to attract or your need on the need stone. You can use a series of stones, one for each letter of the word, and cast them in order into running water. As they fall, see them as part of a mighty rushing river carrying your goal to fruition, and feel the energy surge within you. Keep the stone of self with you for a whole moon cycle, and if necessary repeat the spell. Try to keep the earthly impetus going.

If after three months there are no results, return to the original source of water and ask it if you are asking the right thing. You may be surprised at the answer.

- Stella found she could no longer play tennis, her great love, to a high standard, because after dislocating her right shoulder her arm remained stiff and painful. She missed the world of the tennis club, but could not bear to go along and watch others, and found it hard to replace her passion with any other leisure activities.

Stella's desire was to enjoy tennis again, and she wrote this on her stone of need, one of a pair of black and white 'panda' stones she had brought back as ornaments from a remote beach in northern Canada. She drove to a fast-flowing river in the early morning, and as the first rays of the sun caught the water, cast her stone into the fastest-flowing part of the river. Then she put her stone of self, along with her tennis racquet, in her glass conservatory for a moon cycle.

After a month she went along to the club for the first time, and met Jenny, the daughter of a member. Jenny wasn't at all the usual kind of person to see in the sports-oriented atmosphere. She didn't even enjoy the game herself, and had only come with her mother on this occasion as an observer. Stella noticed that Jenny had a single stone on a cord round her neck that was remarkably like the distinctive black and white stone she had used for her spell.

Stella took Jenny for a drink in the bar, and discovered she was teaching in an inner-city school and was hoping to find players who would give up some summer weekends to teach the children the rudiments of tennis. Jenny was disappointed, however, as her own mother and the other members were only interested in competitions and coaching junior members with a promising future on the tennis circuit. Stella found herself offering to set up a scheme and dragoon other members into helping, but doing much of the coaching herself.

And the stone? Jenny had found it in a local river.

BANISHING SPELLS

Use two stones, one to represent yourself and one the habit or person you wish to remove from your life. You don't want to throw yourself away along with the habit. Do this spell at dusk, on the waning moon, or during the period after the full moon until the crescent is seen in the sky. Again use the stone of self to write what you wish to lose. You can again use more than one stone by writing a word or letter on each, and as you drop each one consecutively into the water see it falling to the bottom of the river or sea and resting there. Walk away from the river or source of water, and keep your stone of self safe for a full month in a drawer or box. Straight after the spell begin a new activity, or go where you will meet new people.

Repeat the spell as necessary over the next two months, and if your craving is strong ask the water source why you still need to hold on to the habit. The answer may not be the one you expect.

• Lucy could not give up smoking, in spite of nicotine patches, hypnotherapy and medication. She hated the habit which she began in her late teens after the death of her mother, and knew it was very damaging to her own health. At 46 she had had several severe bronchial attacks, but her efforts to give up cigarettes always foundered at the first crisis.

She found 11 stones on a shingle beach, one for herself and the other ten to break up the problem into steps. She used the stone of her self to scratch the ten letters of her addiction (cigarettes) on ten stones. It was dusk, the tide had just turned, and Lucy waited for each new flow of tide to cast one of her stones, seeing the craving flowing out of her and the fresh breeze of the sea replacing the choked air of her lungs.

When she returned home she placed her stone of self in a drawer with an empty cigarette packet, and instead of reaching for a cigarette began a typing programme she had had for several months but never used. Lucy lasted 20 days, the longest she had ever gone without a cigarette, before accepting one from a woman at work.

At dusk the same evening, Lucy took out her stone of self and went back to the shingle beach to repeat the spell. This time she threw away even the empty cigarette packet when she got home, and decided to chew gum whenever she felt a craving, and to continue with the typing programme, which she found difficult. However, she knew it would help her to use a computer at work for stock control.

The second month Lucy lasted 25 days before asking a friend for a cigarette, and the same evening she again returned to the sea and repeated the spell, again returning her stone of self to her drawer, and deciding to embark on an exercise routine when the craving became strong.

After 26 days the craving for a cigarette was almost unbearable, but instead of reaching for one, Lucy headed for the beach with her stone of self. The tide was very high, and she asked the waves why she could not give up. The answer came back 'Father'. Lucy hadn't spoken to her father, who was now an elderly man, since she left home at 17. Very soon after her mother's death, her father married a woman he had been meeting secretly while Lucy's mother was very ill. They went

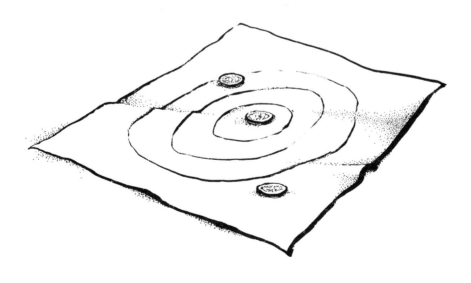

on to have a family, and though Lucy's aunts had indicated many times that her father sought a reconciliation, Lucy had refused even to acknowledge him. Now she realised it was time to resolve the situation and perhaps to forgive.

After arranging a meeting with her father, Lucy realised she had not gone back to smoking, and now very rarely feels the need.

BURYING THE BONE

Often quarrels can go on long after the original issue has been resolved or forgotten. Resentments can harden like stone and positions become entrenched. Burying the bone is an old tradition; as the bone decays, the bad feeling disappears. To bury a stone engraved with the cause of the anger can dissipate the heaviness of grief you may feel. You can place on the spot a herb such as rue for regrets, gillyflowers for affection, peonies for sorrow, honesty for true communication, an almond for hope, lilac, red roses and red carnations for love, gladioli to ease pain, white carnation for affection, white pansies for loving thoughts, or any root flowers or vegetables that will promote new growth from the deeply-buried disagreements.

Do this spell in the evening, so the old regrets may disappear below the horizon with the setting sun. Those old proverbs about not letting the sun set on your anger underpinned this magical concept. For extra power use the days around the dark of the moon period, where the old mingles with the new and promises a new start.

Prepare a hole for your stone, write the old sorrow on it, and as you lower it into the ground see the flame of anger going out. You may wish to light a dark-coloured candle and snuff it out as you cover your stone with earth. Afterwards light a white candle to replace it, and leave that to burn out naturally in a sheltered place, asking the light from it to illuminate both you and whoever you are estranged from. Plant your seed or flowers and take the first steps towards reconciliation, perhaps sending some flowers that are of significance to you both, or some special fruit containing seeds.

If you have a picture of the person from whom you are parted get it out and leave it for the moon cycle, perhaps lighting a white candle for new beginnings or pink for reconciliation each night at sunset, and letting it burn away naturally. You might like to blow it out before you sleep, sending out its love and light.

MAGICAL STONES

Magical wands can be made of stone as well as crystal, and though you can't buy one, there are many around on shores, hillsides and in parks or gardens, that can add strong earth energies to the creative and receptive powers of a clear crystal wand. A stone wand can be useful if you need to take practical steps to achieve any goal. You may also find them reassuring to use since they are so heavily grounded in the earth. To find your stone wand, go for a walk in an open space and see if you can pick one up on what seems to be a well-trodden path or well-washed shore. Low tide on a rocky beach is a good time to find one, but you may equally detect an old water course or ley path even in the most urban recreation ground.

You don't need to be an expert dowser to find one of these 'old ways'. (Dowsing is explained in more detail in Chapter 10.) These ancient routes usually run in straight lines, either between natural markers, particularly prominent rocks on hills or on a plain, or in town running between churches, which were often built on sites of great energy. You may need a street map to find the line, and you can guarantee that unless you're in a US town or city with a grid road system, there may not be a direct route. You'll sense when you are on it by the vibrations you feel within your body as you lock into ancient leys. Along this route you will find your stone magic wand – a stone not more than a few inches long, but quite slim, pointed at one end and rounded at the other.

The creative, 'go for it' energy resides in the pointed end, the gentler, intuitive forces in the rounded. If you want something, or wish to achieve a goal in the outer world, point the sharp end towards the horizon and see a silver energy shoot upwards and outwards. You can use this pointed end for any attracting magic.

The gentler, receptive energy is more like a soft grey mist, and provides reassurance and protection for you and those you love. It is the energy that nurtures both your inner world and your home life, and is good for establishing a secure base for any relationship. If the world is too frantic or your life too noisy and demanding, hold the rounded end of your stone wand between you and the main direction of any intrusion or threat. Feel yourself enveloped in its blanketing calm. You can also use the receptive end of your wand for any banishing magic, remembering to pour any negativity into the earth and counter it by an environmentally friendly action.

FOSSILS AND HOLEY STONES

Because of their immense antiquity, fossils can offer access to a very ancient and permanent wisdom that can be of help in resolving present dilemmas. Stones with holes in the centre, often found on beaches, can also provide a peephole into past ages that underlie the modern world. You may believe that we live only once, or return to some kind of collective consciousness where we don't recall specific lifetimes. Perhaps, however, each life is part of an ongoing learning process, and we can all tap into the past, whether through specific memories or an affinity with certain times and places.

Hold your fossil or look through your holey stone, not just in great castles but in industrial museums, disused factories and urban terraces. History isn't just about old stone circles and warrior queens. Your personal path may be strongest at the turn of the century, in some back-to-back terrace in the north of England. It may be an unromantic, mundane period that can say most about your present needs and problems, so it's vital to stay open to any influences and consider the baronial halls or the Gold Rush as a bonus.

Let any pictures form as they will, whether in your mind's eye or as direct visions, sounds or even smells, whether of home baking or primitive drains. Don't try to rationalise or research the period, except to help you understand the context of your vision. You may find over time that a more general image forms, but sometimes it is the flashes of colour or the sudden sound that can evoke a whole rich inner world that puts your present world picture into context. If you are interested in this concept, it is developed in my book, *Discover Your Past Lives* (Foulsham, 1995).

THE POWER OF CRYSTALS

Crystallos, the clear ice of the Greeks, the crystal of truth, was dropped by Hercules from Mount Olympus and shattered into the millions of pieces of crystal we still use today. So says legend of the clear crystal quartz that has become the term used for other coloured crystalline minerals and semi-precious gems.

Clear quartz was called the essence of the dragon in oriental tradition, and is the frozen white light of the Great Spirit of the Aborigines. Mankind has always had a special reverence for crystals and gems. In early childhood many of us played at fairy crowns with the contents of the button box.

Your crystal wand, pointed and clear at one end and rounded and cloudy at the other, may not be the fairy wand of childhood, but it contains the creative and receptive energies you need for any magic spell. Pointed to the sky, the positive, energising and creative aspect can give pure white light to any new venture or relationship. You know the sky is the limit as you see yourself making those gigantic leaps and steps to whatever constitutes fulfilment.

Facing the earth, the clouded, receptive, nurturing aspect of your wand can help you to abandon redundant stages in your life, to trust your own intuitive wisdom, and to protect yourself and those you love. The gentle white mist can cocoon you and bring peace, healing wounds of the emotions and providing a safety net in sorrow. Sky and earth, *yang* and *yin*, combine in your wand to link you both to the heights of your potential and abilities, and to the depths of your wisdom and compassion. At times you will need to point the clear end of your crystal towards yourself to boost your flagging energies and enthusiasm, and direct the receptive crystal towards the world, to ward off negative influences, and towards yourself, to promote inner calm when you are feeling jagged.

Every colour of crystal has a creative and receptive aspect, a bright, sparkling or densely coloured shade to galvanise active forces, and a softer, translucent or delicately transparent hue for our gentler nature. You may like to make a collection of creative crystals to ring any spell requiring action and new beginnings. Soft receptive crystals can strengthen your spells for reconciliation or moving on. The colour meanings are those already used in the book:

White – is for anything to do with children or babies, and new ventures or beginnings, whether in love or business.

Black – is for letting go of old sorrows, grief or guilt, and for problems with older people.

Brown – is for practical issues, for home and animals.

Pink – is for reconciliation, friendship and health.

Red – is for fertility, survival issues and passion.

Orange – is for identity issues, for personal happiness and partnerships, whether at home or at work.

Yellow – is for communication, for undeveloped potential, for career and for travel.

Green – is for any matter of the heart, for romance, marriage and family.

Blue – is for learning, for examinations, interviews and matters of principle.

Purple – is for wisdom, for the soul and spirit, and for religious insight of any kind.

Because of their natural energies from long years in the earth, washed by rivers or the sea, eroded by the air and transformed by volcanic fire, crystals can provide a rich source of integrated energy to initiate any spell or to offer healing and comfort. Though crystals have attracted great mystique, and complex and often conflicting rules as to their handling, cleansing and using, they are at essence as simple and complex as life itself.

You can choose a crystal you like and keep it with you, safe in the knowledge that its powers will never hurt you. You instinctively form the basis for your own crystal work from your natural intuitions, and respond creatively as you do to any living entity. Just as an animal knows which root or plant will help it in sickness, so you, too, can automatically select the right crystal to heal an ill or soothe a pain. Children use crystals with confidence, and so invariably get the most from them. You can devise your own spells and rituals using them.

A crystal spell for energy

Circle yourself with brightly coloured crystals. A clear crystal quartz offers pure energy and enthusiasm. Rich red, such as a carnelian or red jasper, offers the raw energy to win through. Vibrant orange, such as amber or an orange jasper, asserts that we exist, separate from others, while a sparkling yellow citrine

or golden topaz assures direct, clear communication with self and others, filtering out the negative and destructive.

Brilliant blue crystals, such as dyed blue howzite or lapis lazuli, eye of the gods, can summon courage of mind. Bright green, a malachite or aventurine, may prompt you to speak and to act from the heart. Rich purple, sodalite or sugilite, will offer strength to rise above the material world and its concerns.

Place the crystals in a circle, with white on the top and red to the immediate right of it, followed by orange, yellow, green, blue, and purple to the immediate left of the white. Hold each crystal in turn, beginning with the white, and move round the circle clockwise. Absorb the special energies of each crystal, seeing a shaft of coloured light entering any dark grey corners within, and replacing apathy and lethargy with joy and enthusiasm.

If you don't have the specific colours, use any brightly coloured or sparkling crystals, or even glass buttons, and visualise the rainbow energies circling round you.

CRYSTALS AND THE CHAKRAS

In Chapter 5, on making the workplace psychically friendly, I suggested visualising the traditional chakra colours pouring from your head in ascendancy from dark red to pure white energy.

If you have the crystal colours, you can link with these projected energies. Hold each crystal in turn on the appropriate area of coloured energy within your body – red on the base of your spine for basic power and the will to survive, orange on your pelvis to assert the love you have for your body and pride in your unique identity.

Rest your yellow crystal on your solar plexus, just above your navel, asserting the accuracy of your gut reactions, communicating your desires and needs, assimilating what is of value from your environment and rejecting what is irrelevant or destructive. Place your bright green crystal on your heart; know the truth in your heart and your real priorities.

Blue resides on your throat for speaking that truth and adding the knowledge of the conscious world. Violet between your brows, where the third eye is said to be, gives inspiration, and recognises the wisdom of your unconscious world. Pure white light from the top of your head joins all the other energies in one flowing glorious light beam that flows upwards and downwards. Feel the energies rising and gaining impetus as they join in a spiralling vortex of colour.

After you have used each crystal place it in the original circle formation. Once you have completed the circle, leave it intact in a safe place and go out into the world and use your new-found energies. This is a good sunlight spell.

A crystal spell for calm

Circle yourself with receptive crystals, beginning with a black one such as an obsidian (or Apache tears), or a soft black pebble, for acceptance and self-love. This time explore the circle anti-clockwise, beginning with the black and moving on to the soft purple crystal on its immediate left, feeling all the tensions fading, all the strong feelings being washed away, and the vivid colours of your inner energies being replaced by much gentler shades.

Gentle purple amethyst stands for the world of dreams and visions that can balance the frantic activity of the outer world. Pale blue, such as blue lace agate or a moonstone, mediates principles with compromise, and a realisation that some of the things that seem so important today will have paled into insignificance by tomorrow.

A subtle green jade or moss agate speaks of going with the flow of life and not wasting time on regrets. A gentle yellow crystal, yellow calcite or rutilated quartz, encourages inner communication. A soft pink such as rose quartz offers inner calm, as well as resolving outer conflicts. Finally, to the immediate right of the black crystal, a brown pebble talks of the reassurance of touching home base and knowing what is of value in your life.

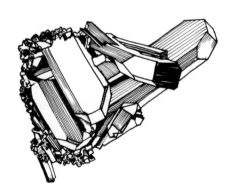

Closing the chakras

You may like to let your black stone close your white energy point at the top of your head, lilac your brow, gentle blue your throat chakra, soft green your heart chakra, pale yellow your solar plexus, pink your pelvis, and brown the root of your spine.

The rising power of the energising crystals can be reversed; you feel the buzzing in your head slowly descend until you have a slight warm heaviness at the base of your spine.

YOUR CRYSTAL REPOSITORY

If you choose a chunk of unpolished crystal, perhaps rose quartz or amethyst, you can use it as a source of energy and wisdom. As this is going to be a constant crystal in your life, you might like to cleanse it under running water; sprinkle it with salt for the earth element; and pass it through a candle flame for fire and the smoke of frankincense – the incense of the sun – and jasmine – the incense of the moon. Let it absorb sunlight and moonlight throughout a moon cycle.

Hold your crystal in your left (receptive) hand when you feel positive, to absorb your energies. When you feel dispirited, sad or jangled, hold your crystal in your right (creative) hand and let it restore the energies and positive harmonies to your body.

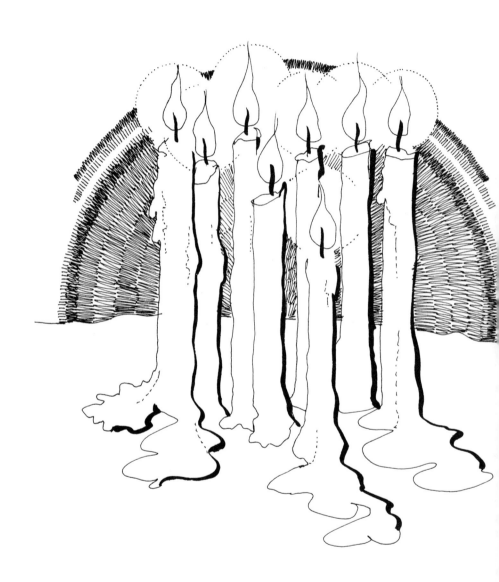

CANDLE MAGIC

From early times candle magic has formed a powerful focus for fire spells of all kinds. Whether you use a white kitchen candle or colours representing your astrological sign and your desires, the power is undiminished. We all lit birthday candles as children and as we blew out the flame knew that our wishes would come true. Now it's just a bit harder. First decide upon your need. Though some people do practise candle magic without a specific focus, it works better if it has a purpose.

THE CANDLE OF YOU

You can use absolutely any candles you wish, but your astrological colour can personalise a candle spell. As always there is disagreement as to these colours, and at the end of the day your instinct is the best guide. However, the most usual associations are:

Aries – 21 March–20 April: Red
Taurus – 21 April–21 May: Pink
Gemini – 22 May–21 June: Pale grey
Cancer – 22 June–22 July: Silver
Leo – 23 July–23 August: Gold
Virgo – 24 August–23 September: Green
Libra – 24 September–23 October: Blue
Scorpio – 24 October–22 November: Burgundy or indigo
Sagittarius – 23 November–21 December: Yellow or orange
Capricorn – 22 December–20 January: Brown or black
Aquarius – 21 January–19 February: Violet or dark blue
Pisces – 20 February–20 March: White

You can light the candle of your zodiacal sign, or if your

birthday is near the cusp, the colour sign closest to your birth date, at any time you need to strengthen your identity or feel under stress.

If your colour does not feel right, choose the candle colour of the zodiacal sign that seems to represent the qualities you crave at present. A list is given below.

As you light the candle, see your essential self, or those qualities you desire, expanding and illuminating your being, giving you confidence, empathy and purpose.

Blow out the candle and send that power emanating throughout your being. Often in candle magic we send love and light to others who need it. Today it is for ourselves, for unless we are strong and happy within ourselves, we cannot give to others.

Zodiacal qualities

Aries offers determination.
Taurus brings patience.
Gemini offers adaptability.
Cancer uncovers hidden potential.
Leo brings courage.
Virgo offers independence.
Libra provides balance and stability.
Scorpio offers clear vision.
Sagittarius provides direction.
Capricorn gives method and order.
Aquarius offers idealism.
Pisces brings sensitivity and intuition.

DRESSING YOUR CANDLES

You may wish to dress your zodiacal candle with a scented oil prior to lighting. I have listed some fragrances in Chapter 4, in the section on tree, herb and flower magic, but below are oils with astrological associations that can be bought from a herbal or New Age shop.

Aries – cedarwood and pine. Cedarwood is useful for all matters of the spirit, and pine for protection.

Taurus – rose and geranium. Rose is for love and geranium (also known as rose geranium) for fidelity.

Gemini – lavender and lemongrass. Lavender is for harmony and lemongrass for magic.

Cancer – jasmine and sandalwood. Jasmine is for good dreams and sandalwood for sexuality.

Leo – orange flower (neroli) and juniper. Orange flower represents happiness and juniper is a protective oil.

Virgo – patchouli and lily. Patchouli is for material success and lily for self-reliance.

Libra – marjoram and magnolia. Marjoram represents insight and magnolia intuitive awareness.

Scorpio – lemon balm and myrrh. Lemon balm is for healing and myrrh for self-exploration.

Sagittarius – rosemary and frankincense. Rosemary enhances memory and frankincense spirituality. Be careful using frankincense unless diluted, as it can be a skin irritant.

Capricorn – cypress and vetivert. Cypress represents letting go of the past and vetivert money.

Aquarius – lemon verbena and coriander. Lemon verbena is for romance and coriander for reconciliation.

Pisces – camomile and ylang-ylang. Camomile represents your inner world and the tropical ylang-ylang sensuality.

As well as an appropriate zodiacal oil, you can choose an oil that complements the purpose of your candle wishes. You can use any of these oils with your zodiacal or other candles to represent the qualities you see in your candle magic; you are not tied to the zodiacal correspondences.

Any of the moon oils are perfect for candle magic, such as jasmine, lemon balm, myrrh and sandalwood, offering the unconscious wisdom and intuitive awareness of the moon. You can try combining oils for joint properties, e.g. orange and camomile combine happiness and the inner world to represent inner joy, and is one of my own favourite combinations.

Alternatively, explore your local New Age shop and see which candle dressing oils match your favourite fragrance or personal associations.

Candle dressing

There are several methods of dressing a candle. The aim is to endow the candle with your essence. My own favourite method is to work in a fragrant oil, from top to bottom, in a spiral, anti-clockwise or in a moonwise direction.

Others prefer to begin from the top of the candle, working sunwise and downwards, left to right to the centre. They then travel upwards and moonwise from bottom to top, right to left, to meet in the centre.

Sarah's zodiacal spell

• Sarah had fallen in love with another man at a stage when her marriage was particularly unhappy. James asked her to leave her husband and go to live with him in his London flat. But although her husband Alan was frequently unfaithful and cold towards her, they had a young son, and James made it clear that there was no place in their future for him.

Sarah's zodiacal candle is white as she was born under Pisces. Like many Pisceans, myself included, she is frequently pulled in two directions.

For this reason, she dressed her candle with marjoram, the oil of Libra, for insight and for the zodiacal quality of balance. She lit her candle as dusk was falling in the waning moon period for unfinished business, and asked that she should be shown the right path. As she stared into the candle flame, her mind was filled with a feeling of vulnerability and uncertainty, and she realised that she was gaining an insight into her young son's feelings.

She left the candle to burn itself away, and when it had done so realised that her relationship with James had run its course. If James could not accept her son, there was no choice, for she could not leave her child. She decided to make one last attempt to save her marriage and improve family life. If this failed, she decided, whatever the cost, to start again alone with her son.

Magic can be remarkably simple, but can put us in touch with the wisdom deep in our soul that may offer solutions. If ignored, however, our actions may cause us to lose our integrity.

THE CANDLE OF YOUR NEED

For many candle ceremonies, a second candle can amplify your zodiacal energies and direct your spells towards a particular area.

White – for any new venture or relationship.
Red – for fertility, sexual matters and survival issues.
Orange – for independence and confidence.
Yellow – for career, any creative adventure and for money.
Green – for love, relationships and health.
Blue – for travel, success in exams and study.
Violet or indigo – for inner happiness and psychic awareness.
Pink – for reconciliation.
Brown – for home and home moves, or any practical matter.

You may find that other colours fit more with your own beliefs; the colours I have suggested are only a guide.

Your candle wishes

Take two candles, your zodiacal colour and one to represent a current area of concern or desire in your life. Use any crystals you may have of the same colour to circle the candles. Some people surround the candles with their jewellery and coins as symbols of wealth, with fruit and vegetables as a symbol of plenty, tiny dolls if love or fertility are involved, and flowers for health, even books if there's learning to be done.

Dress your candle with an appropriate oil according to your need – perhaps your zodiacal candle with an associated zodiacal oil, and the candle of need with an oil that links with the particular strength you desire. As you light each candle see yourself in the desired situation, the person you are now, with all your strengths and failings, happy and complete.

On a piece of paper of the appropriate colour of your need, write your wish and desire. Light the paper in the candle flame of your zodiacal candle and put it on a saucer. If the paper burns entirely then it is said you will fulfil your wish very soon. If it goes out partially burned, then your desire will take longer to come to fruition.

You can leave the candles to burn themselves down and see which burns itself out first. Decide in advance whether you count the last one left burning, as I do, as the key, and if so how you interpret the meaning. If your zodiacal candle is the last one burning, then you may find that you can get help and support from others, but if it is your candle of need, then you will probably have to go it alone, at least in the initial stages.

Candle wishes in reverse

For clearing unwanted clutter from your life, perhaps before embarking on a new venture, house move or even a relationship.

The spell can be carried out just before sunset, when the moon is waning, in your bedroom facing the window, or in a high place, such as a hilltop. It combines the power of sun and moon, day and night, earth and sky, first to remove any doubts and fears and to replace them with confidence, amplified with the energies of the earth, leaving us cleansed and charged for new beginnings.

My own favourite spot for this kind of magic is Five Barrows Down, a series of Bronze Age burial mounds on top of the downs on the Isle of Wight, from which the whole island and the sea surrounding it can be seen.

Outdoors, walk in a spiral step, either alone or with a trusted friend, step, tread, stamp, so that you can feel the vibrations of all who have passed that way before.

If you are indoors you can clap out the rhythm. Match your footsteps or hand-beat with a simple chant such as, 'We are one, the earth is one', louder and faster, facing the highest point, until the sun sinks slowly or the light fades if it is a dull day. You may find that words suggest themselves quite naturally. Move and chant more quietly until twilight has fallen.

Light a small golden or natural, undyed, beeswax candle, and on pale yellow paper write your sorrows or what it is you wish to leave behind to be consigned to the flame.

Burn your candle wish in reverse just before darkness falls. According to tradition, the moon will take our discarded dreams and unfulfilled trysts and hold them deep in her bosom to fall at dawn as healing dew.

On the new moon, plant a small pot of rue for regrets, or parsley for endings, the herb of Hecate, the night crone. As they grow, new life will flower.

A candle spell for galvanising inner powers before an examination, interview or important meeting

In ancient times, when people lived by the sun and moon and worshipped them, in the face of frequent death there was only the belief that life would go on, that spring would follow winter, the tides would continue to rise and fall, the moon would rise, reach its ripeness, wane and be reborn. The maiden would become the mother, the mother the old wise woman, who would die like the moon, but with the promise of rebirth and life renewed.

Wiccans have a ceremony for bringing down the moon, linked with the idea of the triple lunar goddess – maiden, mother and crone – that corresponds with the main phases of the moon. However, the idea translates equally into the concept of using the moon as a symbol for our own latent energies.

Carry out this spell on the first clear night of the full moon, or at any time you need it, immediately after dusk.

Light eight candles, four each of scarlet and white, for energy and action, alternately at the main compass points around a circle, so there is a scarlet candle to the north, east, south and west of the circle.

Draw or cut from silver foil a crescent moon shape for the waxing moon (the crescent shape to the right for the waxing moon), and place this in the centre of the circle. On it, place the red candle from the north, and see all the new energies surging within you, optimism, enthusiasm and stirring excitement.

Now cut or draw a full gold moon and replace your crescent with this, adding the red candles from the east and south. See the power rising within you, directed, joyful, seizing and maximising the opportunity.

Remove the full moon and place the crescent moon shape to the left this time to represent the waning moon; see yourself resting, successful, happy and waiting for energy to return for a new beginning. Add the final scarlet candle from the west. As you blow your four central candles out, send your wishes for success into the cosmos and light to all those who criticise you and try to divert you from your course.

Leave the full moon symbol with the crescent horizontally upwards, facing across it, and the four white candles in south-east, south-west, north-west and north-east positions, to burn out naturally. If you have a clear quartz crystal, place this in the centre on top of the moon shapes until morning.

A candle love spell

The mirror was said to reflect the soul, and many of the old love spells involve projecting the image of a loved one or lover-to-be on to a mirror by candlelight.

Set a table in front of a mirror. Find something made of copper, the metal of Venus, classical goddess of love. If you have nothing else, a two-pence piece can symbolise copper, since coins used to be made of copper. Copper is believed to attract love or friendship. The rose is both the flower and incense of Venus, so use a red rose for blossoming love and a rose incense.

Use a green and a pink candle, the colours of Venus. Light your rose incense and candles of love, and between them place your rose, copper and any crystals.

Light first your pink and then your green candle for growing love, seeing your love unfolding like a flower. Brush your hair, a way of soothing your conscious mind, and as you do so see the image of your lover or projected lover in the candle flame, reflected through the mirror. Send loving thoughts to this known or unknown partner, and ask in your heart that if it is right you will have the opportunity to meet.

You are not summoning up anyone's soul, but merely projecting an image from your deep unconscious. You may see nothing in your mirror, only in your mind's eye, but this is just as good. You may be surprised that the image is of someone quite ordinary. Let the candles burn away naturally. If you have a prospective partner, wear or carry your copper when you next

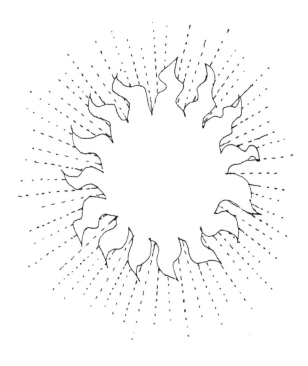

go out, or wear it until the right person comes along. Fill your life with earthly activity and you will be surprised that love comes when least expected. There is someone out there for all of us if we are realistic and look for a person and not an idealised relationship.

A candle spell for reconciliation

Whether you have a difficult boss, relation or colleague, candle magic can be a subtle way of sending them positive vibes to overcome what may be a natural negativity or misplaced resentments.

Use a pink candle for reconciliation or a purple or dark blue one for healing wisdom on an unconscious level. Dress your candle with a virgin olive oil for peace, and as you do so soothe your adversary mentally, uttering words of reassurance in your mind. Concentrate on all his or her virtues – everyone has some. As you light your candle, see the person within the flame, smiling and relaxed. Smile back, and now see them extending the hand of friendship or peace. In your mind's eye step into the candle flame holding an olive branch, and see them accepting it. If a person is especially prickly you may need to use a pink and a purple candle, and see the light and warmth illuminating every fibre of their being. Blow out the candle.

If you can, telephone them with a positive message and offer to do a favour or help in some way. If there is any sign of warmth, build on this the next time you meet. If not, repeat the spell at regular intervals.

CANDLE DIVINATION

Make a special candle place in a darkened room, where you can be quiet and undisturbed. Use a dark blue or purple candle and look into the flame, letting your eyes half close. Do not ask a specific question, but let your unconscious mind cast up images. You may see a person, in which case let his or her story unfold and see how it links with your own.

Watch the candle shadows and pictures. You may see your own special image or a series of pictures, either in the candle flame, the shadows cast on the walls or in your mind's eye. The pictures may be far more complex than you get from tea-leaf or herb scrying. Don't try to analyse them; simply let them flow, and when they cease spontaneously, note them down.

If you make a regular candle divination time, you may find

that a consistent figure appears, who may be a spirit guide from deep within you, a higher essence of your own personality, or perhaps some link with past consciousness. Whether or not we believe in past lives, there may be a well of universal consciousness that may find echoes in our present situation.

Maureen's candle divination

• Maureen is in her sixties and has been a widow for several years. The manufacturing business she ran with her husband is now controlled by her son on a day-to-day level, and she has more time for herself. For about six months she has been seeing Ray, a widower. After a very happy holiday together, Ray has suggested they get married, but Maureen's family are very suspicious that Ray is after her money, since he is a retired taxi driver, living in a rented mobile home.

Ray has always insisted on paying for them when they go out, and Maureen feels that her happiness is what matters. Nevertheless, her family have unsettled her.

She lights a candle and instantly sees a gypsy man, selling pots and pans from a caravan. He is offering her his hand, and she sees herself, much younger, getting in the caravan and going off along a narrow road towards the open sea. The next image is of a boat on a calm sea and the sun shining. When the images disappear, Maureen feels sad, as though she has lost something important.

At first the pictures don't make sense, but then she realises that the gypsy is a much younger Ray. Her life has been very conventional; she married young, had two children in the first two years, and as they grew older became increasingly involved in her husband's business. When he died, she settled down to being Grandma, and occasionally going into the business almost as a visitor.

Ray is very different and, she realises, genuinely unconcerned about money and property. He has suggested that they spend six months touring Europe in a motor caravan for their honeymoon. The candle images confirm for Maureen that this is what she actually wants, to break free from the mould of her life. She is prepared to trust her own judgement and for once abandon the safe option.

Candle options

If you have two options, light two candles on a metal tray,

perhaps using blue for logic versus green to follow your heart; red for act, pink to wait; white for go and a dark colour for stay. You can choose your colours according to what feels right, or use a golden candle for the *yang* option and silver for the *yin* option, 'Yes' or 'No'. You can even use it to make a choice between two people or jobs.

As you light each candle, endow all your hopes and fears about each option into the flame. Leave them to burn in your quiet candle place and occupy yourself with pleasant tasks, or simply let your mind roam free in the candlelight, until the first candle goes out or burns down. Sometimes one may go out very quickly, giving you an almost instant answer, but in more complex issues, the choice may not be so clear.

WAX DIVINATION

Wait until the second candle burns down. Look at the shapes formed by the wax on the tray and let the first image, picture, or even words that come into your mind, act as a guide. You may find that the wax images give you an entirely different perspective on your choice. You can also use this method with a single or series of coloured candles, not linked to an option, but burned as candle wishes.

Tricia's wax divination

- Tricia is in her late twenties and has been offered a training course 200 miles from her home. She has just bought a small house, however, and is reluctant to move away now she has the home of her dreams.

However, the course would guarantee her promotion at a time when she has risen as far as she can go in her sales position. A long-standing relationship with Adam has just broken up, but she has friends and family close by, and fears she will be lonely.

Tricia lights a blue candle for her career move and a green one for following her heart and staying where she is safe. The green candle goes out almost at once, while the blue one flares and then burns steadily.

However, she argues that the green candle's wick was inferior and so it went out, although when she tests it the green candle begins to burn steadily. She leaves the green candle to burn, and the green and blue wax form a clear image of bars with a teddy bear inside, a strange image. Then Tricia understands. She has a favourite teddy bear from childhood whom she still cuddles at night. Her relationship broke up because she had been reluctant to move away with her partner, concentrating on buying a house round the corner from her parents and best friend. Adam had argued that she was creating a prison for them, and his final words were 'You can live there with your teddy bear'.

Now she understands. She decides to let the house for six months and go on the course, and has written to her former partner, telling him of her decision, and suggesting they might meet to see whether anything can be salvaged from their long relationship.

A BEDTIME CANDLE SPELL

Light a soft candle in green or pink for love and place it near the window. In its flame see the faces of those you love, and for a moment be close to them. You might get absent friends or family to light a candle at the same time each night wherever they are, and link in love. Blow out the candle and send loving light to every corner of the room to protect you while you sleep.

You can also use this to link in with other women you may not know. I often light a candle at about 9 p.m. UK time, and perhaps some readers might on occasions like to light a candle at this time and link in with positive thoughts of love and peace. On dark winter evenings especially, I often sit and think of all the women around the world who have written to me about their lives and experiences, and I feel less alone.

DOWSING MAGIC

D owsing is a remarkably female-friendly art, and extends far beyond traditional associations of discovering hidden metals or water, to a method of getting in touch with our buried inner wisdom. Indeed the term 'dowsing rod' may derive not from the Teutonic *duschen* (to strike down towards the ground), but the Cornish *dewsys* (goddess), and *rhodl* (tree branch).

Hazel, the tree of wisdom, is the traditional material for a dowsing rod. You can cut a small branch for dowsing. Choose a shape and size with which you feel comfortable, and let it move naturally to guide you along the right path if you are lost, or to find a missing object. Many women feel happier dowsing with a pendulum, however, either a crystal pendulum on a chain, that can be bought quite cheaply from a New Age or gift shop, or a favourite charm on a piece of cord. As I described in Chapter 6, on travelling magic, you can use a key on a piece of string for an impromptu pendulum, but a charm that has personal significance may help you to tune into your inner knowledge. A watch on a chain or a favourite crystal pendant are also good personalised pendulums, but you really can use anything to hand. One of the most effective pendulums I had was a plumb bob on curtain cord.

How does dowsing work? It would seem to involve a form of telekinetic or telepathic power, because some dowsers can locate minerals or water by remote dowsing over a map, which would suggest that the process is not primarily physical. However, many people believe that the earth contains lines of energy, and that stone circles, such as Rollright in Oxfordshire, emit ultrasonic rays as well as radiation and magnetic energies. The pattern of these rays varies according to the cycles of the moon and the seasons. Little is known of the nature of ley lines, or even that they exist in verifiably scientific terms. Nevertheless, there do seem to be certain ways, often straight tracks, perhaps used from Neolithic times, that feel powerful. Whether this is a spiritual rather than a physical energy, or some complex interweaving of the two, I am increasingly aware that it is possible, using a pendulum, to tune into these 'right ways', where some kind of living power of the earth seems to amplify our own inner psychic radar.

Our muscles operate the movement of the pendulum or dowsing rod according to unconscious direction that comes from our inner well of wisdom, and can alert us to the best route or right decision.

As with many psychic skills, I do not believe you can practise in a vacuum, although I know others disagree with me. The way to dowse, I believe, is to use the skill either when you have lost something, or need to make a decision, and so are driven by need and emotion.

DOWSING FOR A LOST OBJECT

- Helen's grandfather lost his travel documents an hour before he was due to leave for the airport to fly halfway across the world to stay with her sister. He could not remember where he put them, and was totally unconcerned. The trip had involved more organisation than it took to get Hannibal and his elephants across the Alps, and Helen was determined they should not fall at the last hurdle.

  She decided to use her pendulum; at crucial moments in the past it had retrieved her children's lost school bags and her car keys.

  The possibilities for the location of a lost object are endless at the best of times. It's all too easy to put shopping away in a hurry and end up with your purse in the freezer and a packet of frozen peas defrosting in your bag.

  Helen started at the last known point, 24 hours earlier, when *she* put the documents in the front pocket of Grandad's case, which was in the hallway. The case itself gave a 'No' response, in Helen's case an anti-clockwise circle, but gave a 'Yes', a horizontal swing like a clock pendulum, at the foot of the stairs, and led her up the stairs.

  In a similar hunt, be prepared for the unusual, and don't try to concentrate or use deduction. If your pendulum swings strongly, search the immediate area, inside, behind and even underneath objects, as well as on the ground. I was once totally fooled in the hunt for my youngest son's coat because he had hung it in the correct place!

  Helen could also have tried remote dowsing, drawing a plan of Grandad's home very sketchily and holding the pendulum over the different areas. The advantage of this method is that you can have a section for 'Not in the home', which can instantly lead you outside. When an area receives a positive response you can use your pendulum to narrow down the options within that area.

Grandad's travel documents turned up in the spare bedroom with his old photograph albums, and the jigsaw fell into place. He had wanted to find some old photos of his wife to take on holiday. Since he didn't want to lose them, he put them with his travel papers, which he had carried upstairs. At that point the doorbell had rung, so he pushed the photos – and documents – back into the box because he was afraid they might get scattered. Then he had gone to get a haircut and met an old friend who had invited him back for tea.

The main problem with hunting for lost objects is doubt, which is why actually searching, as opposed to drawing a map, can get you up and moving, and avoid anxieties and disbelief. There are dowsers who are happy to demonstrate their skills, but I believe that this is very different from using the ability, a gift we all have, in a crisis. Indeed, most remarkable dowsing cases are reported when someone who has never dowsed before, even a child, discovers water in an area of drought when there is an urgent need and conventional methods have failed.

I heard of an order of nuns in the Home Counties who would pray to St Anthony if one of them lost an important article, and shortly afterwards be led to it. The act of prayer may have triggered off their natural dowsing abilities.

If in doubt, retrace your steps from the last time you were aware you had the missing article, remembering not to allow conscious reasoning to interfere with natural intuitive processes. As you follow your pendulum, visualise the context of last holding the object, with all the sounds and smells; a baby's cry or a burning saucepan may trigger off both psychological and psychic awareness, and the missing object will come into view in your mind's eye and in actuality.

DOWSING FOR DECISIONS

Sometimes when we're forced into a quick decision, we can hesitate and doubt the answer that comes into our heads unprompted. If you have a pendant round your neck or a crystal in your pocket, you can hold it and use it as a pendulum, and feel if it vibrates. This would confirm the rightness of your decision. In a meeting you could use a pen, and as you concentrate on the question, feel your improvised pendulum vibrate or remain still. Such an outward confirmation of your gut feeling can be valuable for focusing your inner wisdom.

If you begin with small decisions, you'll build up enough confidence to trust this method for more major issues.

USING A CIRCLE

When there is more time, or if you have to choose between a series of options, draw a circle on a piece of A4 paper, and divide the circle into a number of areas to correspond with different alternatives or solutions.

Before you begin to dowse for a decision, hold your pendulum, whether a crystal or home-made one and, if you have not used a pendulum for decision-making before, ask your pendulum to demonstrate a 'This is the correct choice' response. You may feel your pendulum pulling downwards quite strongly, or becoming very heavy.

As you hold it alternately over the different areas of the circle, move it slowly across the whole circumference, if necessary two or three times. In one particular area you will feel your pendulum pulling very strongly. The area of pressure will probably not be over your conscious choice, and is a quite unmistakable feeling. If you are with a friend, they will also be able to detect the pressure, an advantage if you are consciously trying to guide your pendulum towards what you think would be the easiest solution.

You can use this circle method for career matters, a relationship choice, or even health worries. For health matters, you might like to draw two circles, one for root causes and the other for remedies. Label different areas of the first circle as possible root causes. One area could be organic, one dietary, another stress. In the remedy circle, you could perhaps have alternatives of 'Seek expert help', another for 'Change diet', another for 'Change lifestyle' and a fourth for 'Reduce stress'.

Once you have discovered a possible root cause and solution, you can use your pendulum to soothe any discomfort. Begin by running your pendulum two or three inches from your body, beginning where you feel the tension or discomfort. This may not get any response from your pendulum, as sometimes a headache can have its root in the stomach. Once your pendulum vibrates over the root of the 'dis-ease', however, let it guide your hand over the route of discomfort. Visualise golden healing light penetrating the depths of pain or tension, warming and soothing your whole being.

For more details of this and other methods of pendulum healing techniques, see my book *Pendulum Divination for Today's Woman*, Foulsham, 1994.

Petra's decision circle

- Petra lives in a remote part of Yorkshire and was finding the travelling connected with her new job increasingly difficult. She had to be in London early on Monday morning and often did not return until Saturday. Travel in the winter would be particularly difficult as snow can make the country roads impassable. The firm had been paying for her to stay in a small hotel, but this would soon end. She loved her home, however, and could not bear to live in London. What is more, she could not buy a comparable property there, although the firm had offered to pay removal and legal expenses.

Petra drew a circle and divided it into four equal segments. The first she marked, 'Stay put and carry on with the travelling'. The second she labelled, 'Stay put but get a permanent bedsit', an option she had considered, but which would involve extra expense. The third 'Move to London' she wrote reluctantly. The fourth she labelled, not as she had planned, 'Move outside London and commute', but, to her surprise, 'Find a job in a different field in Yorkshire'. Her previous job had disappeared when the firm she worked for collapsed, and jobs in her specialist field were rare.

Petra moved her crystal pendulum slowly over the circle, having almost decided to move to London. However, the pendulum suddenly became very heavy over the last segment. She tried again but the pendulum was again drawn to the last segment. By the third attempt she was convinced.

For the first time she admitted that she hated travelling and life on the road. But what could she do? She looked in the local paper and saw a job managing a local tourist bureau, at far less money than she was earning. When she added up all the hidden expenses of living away from home, however, she realised that if she economised it would be possible to stay in Yorkshire and enjoy the life she had chosen for herself living in the Dales.

Petra applied for the Tourist Board job and got it.

IDENTIFYING LEYS

It is said that leys run beneath the land in a grid-like system. The most famous British ley line passes from St Michael's Mount in Cornwall to Bury St Edmunds in Suffolk, and is marked with ancient sites, burial mounds, hill forts, stone circles and churches, the latter often built on the sites of ancient pagan places of worship. The significant feature of the St Michael line, as it is called, is that many of the 60 churches along it are dedicated to the Christian saints who replaced the pagan sun gods, St Michael, St George (Og was the Gaelic sun god) and St Mary the Virgin, who replaced the female goddess principle.

Ghostly presences are often explained as a manifestation of abstract earth energies, especially those which appear out of doors or near water. Norfolk, for example, traditionally one of the richest places for ley lines, has many 'natural' ghosts. The road between Gedleston and Bungay is said to be haunted by a phantom coach and horses. At Hickling Broad there is a male ghost who skates across the water, and a white lady has been seen punting at the same spot. He is believed to be a drummer from the Napoleonic Wars, killed as he crossed the water to see his lover.

Horsey Mere, too, is supposedly haunted by ghostly children said to have been interred in water in Roman times; they appear for an hour every year on 13 June. Peddar's Way at Great Massingham is haunted by a phantom black dog, one of many of Norfolk's ghost hounds who haunt the leys.

You can detect ley lines in urban settings as well as country places, using a pendulum. I mentioned these old ways, often running between churches or old official buildings, as a location where you might find your stone wand. The energies of ancient ley lines may evoke images, sounds and even scents of the past, whether your own or those akin to your current life and needs, if you allow your own instinctive powers to guide you.

When you study the history of the area you may well discover sightings of ghosts near the places where the energy was strong – perhaps you saw a few shadows or heard hoofbeats from long ago, sounds and pictures etched in the paving stones, or tracks worn over the years by constant use.

Decision-making using ley lines

You may find that you prefer a more structured approach to decision-making. If so, use a ley line as a focus for a step-by-step approach, using your pendulum.

All you need is a pen and notebook and your pendulum. It may be easier to use urban leys as the landmarks are more varied, although you can equally well ask questions as you walk from hilltop to hilltop, guided by marker stones and clumps of trees.

Find an old area of a town or city. Begin at a market cross, crossroads or civic memorial in the centre of town, where many people will have assembled throughout the ages. The cross may be an old standing stone, Christianised. Where energies intersect, they are doubly powerful.

At your starting place ask your first question quite spontaneously, and write down the answer that comes unbidden. The answer may be a simple 'Yes' or 'No', or more cryptic, a phrase or even an inscription written on the wall that seems relevant. Remember that the best questions for a pendulum are those that ask 'Should I'/'Shouldn't I', rather than seeking to elicit information. By this method you can narrow down the options or discover new avenues, so the answer becomes clear.

Leave the main highways and let your pendulum lead you down narrow streets and alleys. If your pendulum stops or begins to vibrate strongly, pause too. Look around and see what is of significance, a church, a carving high up on a wall, a forgotten garden or choked stream. See if the place offers an insight into your dilemma or decision. Ask your second question, pausing to write the second answer. You may be surprised at the question.

Carry on where your pendulum leads until you have eight to ten questions and answers. You may find you end up where you started quite by chance.

You may find it easier to start outside an old church. The inscriptions on the monuments, a name on a gravestone or a quotation may prompt either your question or answer. For now, do not analyse; simply write down whatever words seem appropriate. When you have finished, go somewhere quiet for a drink and read through your questions and answers. You may find the question you answered wasn't one you even realised was troubling you.

Lydia's ley decision-making

- Lydia is in her forties and has applied for a business loan to run a textiles unit from a workshop in converted warehouses to provide a retail outlet. However, she has been refused a full loan by her bank, and has to raise several thousand pounds for equipment.

She stands with her pendulum underneath the medieval town gate, deserted in the early evening. Her first question is 'Should I give up?' Her pendulum swirls in a negative response. She walks down a narrow alleyway called Spice Alley, and although the shops are shuttered and are almost all bookshops, she can smell exotic spices and fragrances that remind her of an oriental bazaar. Years ago the town was a busy port that traded with the East, and she feels the spices are assuring her that it is right for her to trade to help replace the industry that has died. The pendulum stops by a doorway, above which is an elaborately carved elephant.

'Persistence' is a word that comes into her mind, and she asks, 'Should I try another bank for finance?' Again the pendulum responds in the negative. However, the solidity of the stone elephant suggests to Lydia that her project is a solid one, and could make a steady income.

She walks on, but the pendulum diverts down a row of industrial cottages, now converted into flower-decked dwellings. It stops beside a restored pump, shining bronze with a brass handle. Water, fresh input. Is that what she needs? She asks, 'Should I find an additional source of funding?' This time, the pendulum's answer is positive.

The pendulum seems to be pulling her under a dark archway, which does not seem frightening, but protective. 'Should I take a personal risk to find the money?' 'No', the pendulum is quite definite.

Now the pendulum takes her past an old charity school, with a statue of a girl in blue. The engraving is faded but seems to suggest that the school was a local Charity Commissioners Board School, founded in 1896. Ask for charity? It doesn't make sense. How could charity help a business? Lydia has no benevolent relatives or friends to assist, but the pendulum has been definite. 'Should I get help from a charity?' The pendulum says she should.

Lydia carries on towards the river, but stops at a small church with a single altar. On the wall is a plaque, 'Seek, and ye shall find. Ask and it shall be given.' Ask who? 'Should I look locally for a charity?' The answer is again positive.

Lydia is getting tired and decides to head back to the centre of the town for a drink. The pendulum urges her forward, however, down the cobbled alley to the river. Immediately ahead is a converted warehouse and small pine workshop. Above it is a small plaque, 'Established with the help of ...' and the name of a large manufacturer. A charity? 'Should I contact the firm?' The final answer is 'Yes'.

The next day Lydia, feeling foolish, contacts the manufacturing firm, which tells her it had a Trust Fund, established by the original owners in the early 1920s, to help deserving young apprentices under 23 set up in the furniture or textile businesses. Since the firm now had few apprentices, the scheme had fallen into disuse, but the Charity Commissioners had very recently agreed to widen the terms of the original bequest. The pine workshop was the first beneficiary, and the firm is monitoring its progress before advertising the scheme. However, they offer Lydia a grant from the charitable trust, and promise to help her with her marketing, in return for a right to first option on some of her designs each year.

PSYCHOMETRY

Established psychics claim to be able to tell the history of an object and its former owners by holding it. This power is an extension of natural dowsing ability, and while we may not ever wish or feel sufficiently confident to demonstrate psychometric powers in public, we can all use ancient places and artefacts to trigger off our intuitions. The images we receive when we hold an old piece of jewellery, a stone from a medieval abbey or even a crystal found on the shore may be vague, but they can give us pictures from the past which may find echoes in our present.

Let an object or place choose you. Don't use something a friend has given you, of which they know the precise history. Psychic guessing games are of limited value, and may actually block the information the vibrations of the past can provide.

Hold the object, or a piece of stone you may have found, lightly in both hands. Close your eyes so that your fingers connect with the texture, and then below the surface with the essence. In your mind's eye, place the object in its most natural setting, that may go back many years or just a decade or so. Move outwards and beyond the artefact to its context, letting any fragrances, sounds or colours add to your perceptions.

Alternatively, slowly move your pendulum around it, stopping at any point that seems particularly powerful. Accept any images that come into your mind, and do not be influenced by what you already know or think you should be feeling.

Psychometry and decision-making

If you are worried or trying to decide a course of action, go somewhere where you can handle a variety of objects, a craft or antiques fair. Sometimes a replica of an ancient craft, such as a corn dolly, can carry a legacy of use down the generations. You can hold a family treasure or go to an old ruined church or castle and pick up one of the stones. Remember to return it afterwards to its natural home.

As you run your hands or pendulum over the artefact, ask the question that you wish to answer. First absorb all the impressions you are receiving, either through your mind or projected beyond you, and as soon as you can, note them down. When you cease to receive any more impressions, ask 'Yes' or 'No', 'Go' or 'Stay'. Either hold the object (you may feel a strong vibration if 'Yes' and nothing for 'No'), or let your pendulum swing above the artefact and give you either its 'Yes' response or a 'No'. If you can't get an answer or the response is not definite, you may need to rephrase the question.

The impressions can explain or mitigate the answer. Let your intuition explain what they mean, and don't apply logic.

Julie's psychometry decision

• Julie is married with three children and has been working part-time at the children's school, helping a little boy with special needs. The headteacher has suggested that Julie trains as a teacher of children with special needs, as she has an instinctive, empathic approach to children, although she has received no training.

Geoff, her husband, is very unhappy about Julie going back to college. The grant will not match her wages, and he fears she will be so busy studying she won't have time to look after him and the children. Geoff works long hours and gets very upset if Julie has to go to evening meetings.

Julie holds her pendulum above a Victorian brooch that has been in her family for generations. She feels an intense frustration, a bird in a gilded cage, and senses a young woman trying to escape from a hot room into the fresh air. Then she sees in her mind's eye a door on heavy hinges very slightly open. She is small now and pushing very hard, until a gap appears and she is outside in a huge paved yard. The door shuts behind her; she realises she is alone and that it is beginning to rain. A tall old lady offers her an umbrella, but she refuses. She runs out of the yard and along a cobbled street, and then is flying high like a bird, and very, very happy.

'Should I ignore Geoff's wishes and go to college?' Her hands vibrate very uncertainly around the object, which she takes as a positive response, but acknowledges that such a decision would not be easy and would have many repercussions on the family.

Julie decides to ask the brooch a second question, not one she had expected. 'Should I start in a small way?' This time the positive response is definite. What of the impressions from the brooch? Julie could apply the bird in the gilded cage and the sensation of being confined to her own situation. The family is not short of money, but Julie feels unfulfilled in her home and work life. The huge doors suggested it would not be easy to change the status quo, but the children are growing older and less dependent, and if she perseveres she could very gradually open the door to a more satisfying future.

Being alone and afraid in the rain reflected how much she relies on Geoff for approval and support, and to some extent on the headmistress at school, perhaps the tall lady with the umbrella. Once she began to run by herself it became easier, until at last she was happy and free.

Julie decides to take everything one step at a time. She arranges for her friend to collect the children from school one day a week and cut down her hours, so she is able to attend college in the daytime for a day and a half every week. The courses immediately available are computing and maths; the latter was her favourite subject at school. In time she hopes to qualify for a grant to take a maths and computing degree, perhaps with a view to teaching older children.

She never discovered whether her brooch was owned by someone who made a bid for freedom. That is not important, however; what matters is that Julie was able to use it as a trigger for her own wisdom, rather than following the advice of others.

...•º*DREAMS*º•...

♡ LOVE ♡

HERBS

Agrimony

Used to cure snake bites.

'It draweth forth thorns & splinters of wood, nails, or any other such thing gotten into the flesh.'

A tea made from agrimony flowers with lemon added was used to cure colds.

It was originally used for flavouring beer.

WHERE NEXT?

T he traditional name for a witch's magic book is *The Book of Shadows*, a gloomy if esoteric name for an exciting, living reflection of positive magical energies. The idea of writing down spells, remedies and rituals is one attributed to practitioners far into the mists of time. In reality, such records for private family use, containing old herbal remedies and folklore, would only have been made by women versed in reading and writing – until the beginning of this century quite a small proportion. Records kept by monks and male students of herbalism and folklore tend to be more impersonal, revealing little of the dreams and private lives of those who handed down the treasures of natural wisdom.

Many of the old stories, legends and rituals would have been handed on by practice and word of mouth, and in remote parts families today still jealously guard their special remedies and rituals.

In the modern world, written records of personal magical explorations offer permanence in busy, changing lives, and reflect women's growing awareness of their own spirituality and connection with the past and the natural world. A computer does not offer the same endowing of personality as words written late into the night or early morning, recording love, hopes, dreams and anxieties.

KEEPING A BOOK OF MAGIC

You may choose to buy a bound volume of blank pages to record your magical workings. Choose a large size, A4, with plenty of room to draw circles for dowsing and divination. You can also buy leather-bound folders that look like books, in which blank pages can be inserted. These have the advantage that you can categorise and modify rituals, changing the shape of your collection to fit your new discoveries.

At a later date, you can take a series of loose pages to a bookbinder and have then cased in cloth or leather, which need not be prohibitively expensive. You could print or decorate your own cover.

Whatever your book, whether simple or elaborate, decorated with gold leaf or dried flowers, silver stars or dark velvet, you can keep within it not only lists of your favourite herbs, fragrances, spells and symbol systems, but also dried flowers from a special outing, a small twig in the shape of an animal found on the forest floor, and a tiny stone or shell, polished smooth, offered by the sea after a ritual. You may wish to have a special folder for your natural treasures, or keep them within your magical treasure box.

In Chapter 2 I suggested starting a magic box, and at the end of this chapter I will summarise a list of suggested materials that you may find useful to have in your box, to enable you instantly to carry out most basic magic. It is fun to improvise and, as I have said, the magic resides within us; we can do magic absolutely anywhere with anything. Increasingly, however, I have become aware that personally chosen candles, incense and crystals are a precious addition to everyday magic, a marking out that this is a special time and area of your self that is worthy of time and attention. Like a lot of woman, I do not hesitate to buy presents for my family and friends, but still feel a pang of guilt if I spend money on crystals, incense or a pendulum.

MAKING A MAGICAL BOOK

You could use a pen and black ink, and perhaps a gold marker for the sun, silver for the moon, red for fire, blue for water, yellow for air and green for earth.

Begin with a list of your aims, long- and short-term. You can tick each one as you achieve it, delete and modify as appropriate, and add new ones. You could choose a different theme each month or season.

You could divide the book into sections, based on general categories, perhaps similar to the chapters in this book, or in categories that fit better with your own interests and explorations. Possible divisions might include:

- Herbs, flowers and trees
- Crystals and stones
- The home – protection, spells and divination
- Magic out of doors
- Workplace magic
- Travelling – magic and protection

- Lunar and solar spells
- The seasons and old festivals
- Candle magic
- Pendulum dowsing

In each section, note any special tools or ingredients you have found especially helpful, any rituals you have devised, words that seem effective for you, and symbols that you use in your magic.

Your seasonal section can reflect any special rituals you carried out on the old festivals, such as the longest day, flowers you planted or used to decorate your house, candles and crystals you lit. It can be a reminder of the older, slower world that still turns.

You might have a section near the back, purely as a diary, divided into seven-day periods to which you can add the date and time of day you carried out your spells.

Each time you try some divination, such as a tea-leaf reading, you can write down your initial questions and the results with little sketches in this section, noting how it fits in with what is happening in your life. You can also record your reading in the appropriate section so you can trace the path of each method and see which you find most effective.

Cross-reference with your seasonal, lunar and solar celebrations, noting the phases of the moon if they seem relevant (you can find these in most newspapers each day). You may find that your own cycles gradually move closer to those of the moon. This cross-referencing in the diary section can be a good way of pulling together all the different strands. It can be quite revealing to read through old entries and see how far you have progressed in creating your personal magical system.

Have a section for your own unique symbols, those that appear in dreams, daytime visions and in readings. Note briefly the meanings that seem right for you; these may change over time, so leave space by each for the modified meanings. In the margin put a column for the number of times each symbol appears, and after two or three months you can draw up an alphabetical table of the 50 most prevalent symbols in your divination, across all the different forms you use.

Place the remaining symbols, that have appeared only two or three times over the months, on a subsidiary list. You may find over time that some of the main symbols disappear and new ones or those from the second list take precedence.

Your personal symbol, the image that appears most, especially in times of crisis or major change, may be one that has featured since your childhood, or has appeared since you were married/divorced, or as a result of a life re-direction. You may find that after six months even this symbol is evolving.

Finally, list separately those special moments – when you woke just before dawn and saw the waning moon in the sky with the scarlet light of day creeping to overtake it, a spider's web dripping with diamond dew after rain, the first snowdrop pushing through the frozen earth, the light shafting ancient stones or barrows on the longest day, the sun dancing in a stream at Easter. Some of these you may have listed in other parts of the book, but this section can be immensely uplifting to read if you do feel negative or sad, a reminder that the universe is very special and that you, too, are chosen to play a unique part.

YOUR TREASURE BOX

Mine is a huge plastic container. Yours may be far more special – a wooden box with brass hinges, a box covered with shiny foil and sequins, or painted with flowers.

You can buy your box from an antique shop or car boot sale. If it has been used before, hold it and make sure it feels friendly, and perhaps keep one of your special protective crystals, such as a garnet, jasper or bloodstone, inside it for a while. Wash the crystal under running water and leave it in the sunlight afterwards to regain its positivity.

When you have made or bought your box, which should be at least a foot square and the same in depth, larger if you wish, you can carry out a blessing ceremony. This is not essential, but it can mark your box as a special part of your life.

A treasure box ceremony

Place a dish of salt in the due north (12 o'clock) point on top of your box. Pass the dish around the box, sprinkling each of the corners, and see your box protected by the reassuring energies of the Earth, your magic rooted in the real world, with solid foundations that will ensure success.

Next, light two incense sticks, one of jasmine for the moon and one frankincense for the sun. Beginning in the east, pass the incense around the four corners, seeing the power of air, in which all things are possible, adding infinite potential to your magic.

In the south, place a pure beeswax candle for fire. Pass it round the four main directional points, seeing inspiration and creativity overcoming any obstacles in your path.

Then, in the west, take a dish of rose water or another diluted fragrance. As you pass it around your box, sprinkle the fragrant water in the four corners, recognising in yourself the power to move forward and interpret your deepest intuitions.

Some people prefer to begin each element in the north, but by starting each at its natural home you can provide overlapping circles of energy. Move round the box sun- or clockwise.

Finally, take off the lid, and tracing its edges and corners anti-clockwise with a dark crystal, see all the magic collecting like cotton wool in the base of the box to protect your tools and artefacts.

Using your box

You may wish to keep your box private, for use only when you are alone or with close friends. I used to allow my children free access to my magical things, and in principle this has proved the right decision, as it has destroyed any fears that I am using anything other than natural processes. However, this can mean that things get scattered and I have to search for what I need, a hazard if you live in a crowded household rather than alone. So I mark some limits even with my utilitarian plastic treasure box.

Line it with a dark silk scarf or a natural material if this seems right for you. You can have tiny boxes, bags or purses for your crystals so they do not become scratched. Many miniatures, whether tiny candles, canisters of tea, ancient coins or small china ornaments, suitable for magic, can be bought on holiday or in gift departments of big stores.

The following items, together with the contents of your kitchen cupboards, drawers and tool-box, should be sufficient for most spells and rituals.

- Thin cord in black, white and perhaps one or two other colours, for knot magic and to make an improvised circle and pendulum.
- A small pair of scissors for cutting the cord, and to serve as the sharp air element.
- A small quantity of pot-pourri in a small container with a lid, ready to double as the earth element.

You could be really ingenious and make a pot-pourri from the loose kind sold in some department stores, to represent the seven main planets and heavenly bodies, or buy tiny quantities of each fragrance in little muslin purses:

- Marigold for the sun
- Geranium for the moon
- Lavender for Mercury
- Rose for Venus
- Carnation for Mars
- Honeysuckle for Jupiter
- Mimosa for Saturn

In the old and still frequently practised system, before Neptune, Uranus and Pluto were added, the seven planets ruled the 12 zodiacal sun signs, so you can use these for your birth signs if you don't have time to buy your own personal fragrance:

- The sun rules Leo
- The moon rules Cancer
- Mercury rules Gemini and Virgo
- Venus rules Taurus and Libra
- Mars rules Aries and Scorpio
- Jupiter rules Sagittarius and Pisces
- Saturn rules Capricorn and Aquarius

- Tiny pots of herbs for divination.
  The dried variety can be bought in small plastic containers. Go for two of the traditional divinatory herbs, making sure they are not too powdery:

  - Parsley (Saturn)
  - Sage (Jupiter)
  - Rosemary (the sun)
  - Thyme (Mercury)

  These can also represent the earth element.

- Four candles, which need not be large, and small candle holders (I once made a holder out of the top of an ice-cream sauce bottle in an emergency).
  A plain undyed beeswax candle will serve for any kind of spell, especially those of new beginnings. The following are also useful to keep in your box:

  - Gold for the sun
  - Silver for the moon
  - White, which can be a household candle for any kind of spell, especially for energy

- Incense sticks (optional).
  These can be used in any fragrance. A light floral incense, available in most department stores, can give a room a delicate fragrance. You can keep a selection in your box, as they take little room:

- Frankincense for the sun
- Jasmine for the moon
- Rose for all love spells (Venus)
- Magnolia for the Earth
- Lavender for air
- Cedarwood for fire
- Sandalwood for water

These can all double up for the air element.

- Cook's matches. These can also double up for the fire element.

- Small bottle of still mineral water for the water element. (You can substitute rose water or your favourite essential oil.)

- A pendulum.
    If you buy a crystal one, choose real crystal. Lead crystal is just as expensive and lacks the natural energies. However, you can equally well use any of the suggested substitutes, such as a favourite charm on a cord.

- A small mirror or torch for all kinds of fire and solar magic.

- A tiny battery fan for air magic and divination.

- A packet of fast-growing seeds such as cress, and a little cotton wool to place on a saucer for improvised bedding. This is useful in divination.

- Crystals.
    - Either a quartz crystal wand, clear at one end, cloudy at the other, or two separate quartz crystals, one clear and the other milky, for energy spells.
    - A dark crystal for protective magic, such as a smoky quartz, a dark banded agate or an obsidian; if you hold this last crystal up to the light, you can see through it.
    - A bright red crystal, such as a carnelian or red jasper, for action spells.
    - A sparkling orange crystal, such as amber or orange jasper, for identity spells.
    - A sparkling yellow crystal, such as a citrine or golden-yellow tiger's eye, for communication spells.
    - A soft green crystal, such as jade, for spells concerning love.
    - A bright blue crystal, such as dyed blue howzite or a lapis lazuli, for spells where you need to be logical.
    - A soft purple crystal, such as an amethyst or sodalite, for spells concerning your inner world.
    - A gentle pink crystal, such as rose quartz, for reconciliation and friendship spells.

- A brown crystal, such as a tiger's eye or fossilised wood, for practical and money spells.

  You can manage without the coloured crystals, using a clear crystal quartz as a substitute for any or all. However, you may like to build up a small crystal collection for your personal use.

- A beach or urban stone collection.

- A holey stone.

- A stone wand, pointed at one end, rounded at the other.

- A fossil for connecting with the past.

- A small shell to hear the sea when you are far inland.

- Dark and light pebbles from the beach, for attracting and banishing magic.

- Small symbols – toys, charms or tiny china ornaments. I would suggest a small house, a small plane, boat, car, two or more tiny dolls, an animal, a tiny book and a few copper and silver coins, for spells and divination.

- A quantity of A4 paper, both white and coloured, and pens to draw impromptu circles and write out wishes.

These are a few of my suggestions. You will already have articles you use, and over time you will add to your collection, according to the way your magic develops.

AFTERWORD

P arking spaces, career and relationship problems can become challenges, given magic to help us through. We are like icebergs and barely use the tip of our hidden powers. You may find you want to go on to more formal magical books and practices or, like the majority of women, use magic as a part of the everyday world.

Some women embrace incense, flowers and ceremony as outward expression of their inner powers. Others are happiest scrying in a washing-up bowl or using a fresh-air spray to represent the air element. This book offers no more than suggestions, and as you start to use natural symbols, albeit in their everyday forms, you will surprise yourself with your ingenuity and creativity.

There are no magic answers, no free lunches, no short-cuts to fulfilment. I end this book with a streaming cold, a raging overdraft and a leaking washbasin. I feel more harridan than high priestess as I look in dismay at the pile of washing, and the leaden skies.

But magic begins when reality threatens to overwhelm joy, when confidence fades and doubts fill the hours before dawn. Magic is about laughter, about tears, about being women, trying so hard to do it all and yet exist, free and loved, loving and yet complete in ourselves.

We all have unique strengths, and whether we are conventionally successful, brilliantly 'off-the-clock', or prefer to go from A to Z by the highways and by-ways, enjoying the sunshine and the daisies, we can all discover happiness in our own way. So rev up your Porsche, your battered old Mini, your ten-ton lorry or even the hoover if you've no other transport, and let your magic carry you to wherever destiny takes you.

Smile wherever you are – the woman next to you may well be a fellow witch. It's more than likely. After all, *every* woman is a witch.

INDEX